Business in Clinical Practice: How to Get There from Here

DIANA H. HOPKINS-ROSSEEL
& BRADLEY ROULSTON

Ottawa 2007

First Edition, 2007

Published by
CAOT Publication ACE
Ottawa, Ontario

Copyeditor: Lyne St-Hilaire-Tardif, Lyne's Word

Graphic Designer: Ghina El- Koussa, gkoussa@hotmail.com

Cover Design: Bryan Babcock, Bryan Babcock Design

Illustrations: Thomas H. Rosseel

Copies may be purchased from:
The Canadian Association of Occupational Therapists
CTTC Building
3400-1125 Colonel By Drive
Ottawa, Ontario K1S 5R1 Canada
Tel. (613) 523-2268 ext. 242
E-mail: publications@caot.ca
Through our on-line store at www.caot.ca

CAOT PUBLICATIONS ACE

© Canadian Association of Occupational Therapists 2007

ISBN: 978-1-895437-78-2

Diana's Acknowledgements

One has to wonder if anyone ever reads the acknowledgements at the front of a book. I really, really hope so because there are so many people to thank – many of whom may not know who they are – who have all participated in some way and always at their own cost in time, travel, lost revenues, and sharing of original professional or academic knowledge.

Thank you very much to …

The behind the scenes investors:
Wendy E., Pamela, Bruce, Philip, John, and Nick.

The Community Cardiac Rehabilitation Centre teams:
Larry, Gina, Lyle, Cathy, Bill, Mike, Michelle B., Hans, Lucille, Jane, Patricia, Anita, Wendy S., Kate, Tasleem, Debra K., and *especially* Wendy E., Gloria, Marjan, Michèlle, Tony, Gary, and Glorianne.

The business course advisors, instructors, and expert guest speakers:
Alice Aiken, Edward Bergeron, Anne and Martin Blaser,
Dorothy Borovich, Yvonne Chan, Alan Cosford, Peter Gallant,
Al Guiguere, Frank Gielen, Signe Holstein, Gerry Hopkins, John Johnson,
Steve Lawless, Scott MacIness, Jenny Nelson, David Notman, Vickie Poffley,
Steven Presement, Joe Putos, Bradley Roulston, Peter Schell, Anne Symes, Mike Taylor,
Clarence Willms, and Carolyn Whyte.

The multitude of "Community Advisors" to the students of the business course:
Alice Aiken, Michael Adamcryck, Alison Brown, Barbara Caldwell, Alan Cosford,
Lynn Crowe, Lindsey Fair, Peter Gallant, Maggie George, Al Guiguere, Mark Hanley,
Brian Hogan, Gerry Hopkins, John Johnson, Steve Lawless, Dick Lee, Cathy Louis-
Thrower, Scott MacInnes, Verna Mann, Karen Megaffin, Jenny Nelson, David Notman,
Bob Pritchard, Joe Putos, Terry Romain, Peter Schell, Mike Taylor, Phil Thom,
Susan Thurlow, and Clarence Willms.

The "collaborators" and co-authors:
Bradley Roulston, Mark Edmonds, Peter Schell, Mike Landry, and Alice Aiken.

For the students and by the students

P.S.: Elephant Shoes J, B. and T.

Primary authors
DIANA H. HOPKINS-ROSSEEL
BRADLEY ROULSTON

Contributing authors
Alice Aiken
Mark Edmonds
Mike Landry
Peter Schell

Business Plan authors
Cindy Brown
Nicole Gill
Erin King
Shelley MacRae
Nicole Zwiep

Content editors
Susan Scott Swanson
Kathy Van Benthem

Organizational Support
Funding and support provided by the Canadian Association of Occupational
Therapists for the publication and promotion of this document.

DIANA H. HOPKINS-ROSSEEL
DEC, BSc(PT), MSc(Rehab), MCPA

Diana Hopkins-Rosseel graduated from the University of Toronto in 1982 with a B.Sc. in physiotherapy following three years as an undergraduate science student at Queen's University. Diana then practiced as a fulltime physiotherapist at St. John's Rehabilitation (Toronto), the University of Massachusetts Medical Center (Worcester, Massachusetts) and Hotel Dieu Hospital in Kingston, Ontario until 1989.

As a young physiotherapy clinician working through service rotations at UMass Medical Center, Diana was introduced to cardiac rehabilitation. Since that time she has dedicated much of her clinical and research time to pursuing this area of practice. It was in this rehabilitation setting that she began to investigate behavioural modification theories and their application to improving rehabilitation outcomes.

In 1987 Diana accepted a part-time faculty position in the School of Rehabilitation Therapy at Queen's as a Lecturer while continuing practice in critical care as the Senior Inpatient Physiotherapist at Hotel Dieu Hospital. After successfully completing her Master of Science degree in Rehabilitation in 1991, Diana became a fulltime Assistant Professor and now holds the position of Associate Professor teaching cardiorespiratory physiotherapy, basic clinical skills, professional issues and business practice for clinicians. Over the years she has received many awards for excellence in teaching, among them the Queen's University Faculty of Health Sciences Education Award and the Barbara Edwardson Lectureship at the University of Western Ontario.

In 1987 Diana started a small scale cardiac rehabilitation service in Kingston with a Tourism and Recreation grant. In 1998, after running the Community Cardiac Rehabilitation Centre as a private practice for several years, Diana approached the three public health institutions in town to take over the centre. Diana continues to practice in the Centre at Hotel Dieu Hospital, and in acute care at Kingston General Hospital as a casual physiotherapist.

Diana has also been extensively involved in professional organizations at the local, provincial and national levels. These have included Chair of the Cardiorespiratory Division of the Canadian Physiotherapy Association, Chair of the National Asssociation of Clinical Educators in Physiotherapy, membership on the Board of Directors of the Ontario Physiotherapy Association (OPA) and President of the Quinte-St. Lawrence District of the OPA. Diana has also participated in the development of the bank of questions for both the written and clinical components of the national clinical competency examinations.

Diana's interests extend beyond physiotherapy and the academy. She loves to jog and read fantasy novels, trains and competes on a masters-level rowing team, was co-leader of a local youth group and sings as a tenor in Open Voices, a 120-member, mixed-voice community choir.

BRADLEY ROULSTON
BA, CFP, CLU, RHU

Bradley Roulston, BA, CFP, CLU, RHU. Bradley is a Certified Financial Planner, the youngest in Canada when he received his license. Bradley writes the financial/benefit column for several Health journals including the Physiotherapy Today and Directions. Due to his popular financial planning strategies and volunteer work, Bradley has appeared on the covers of several national financial magazines, has been featured in many articles, as well as been interviewed on numerous TV and radio programs. He operates companies that specialize in financial planning for healthcare professionals as well as being a manger of the Nelson & District Credit Union. Bradley has developed a very comprehensive approach to personal finance, with an eye to social and environmental responsibility.

Foreword

Why a book on starting a private practice and personal finances, and why this type of book? The obvious answer is that such a resource for private practitioners, or private practitioner hopefuls, does not exist in Canada. That is not the whole answer to these questions, though, and perhaps it avoids the good, the bad, and the ugly of any business endeavour, including this one. Therefore, to answer these questions I am going to ramble a bit and take you through a long story, the story of my beginnings in business in health care private practice and in academia, and then make the not so natural link to this book ...

Almost 20 years ago I asked my "boss," the director of the rehabilitation department of a public hospital, if I could start a cardiac rehabilitation program. His answer was "Sure. Put together a proposal, including where the funding will come from, and bring it back to me." I was so naïve; I had no idea what a huge task he had, seemingly so lightly, let me get myself into.

After two years of proposals to regional health authorities and the Ministry of Health, and endless meetings with government officials and health care administrators, I had to admit that public funding would not be right around the corner.

So ... I pulled up my socks and started a cardiac rehabilitation service – with the help of Dr. Larry Wolfe, Professor, Physical Education Department, Queen's University – using a one-time, one-year, Ministry of Tourism grant, free space in the Physical Education Centre, and free labour. It only took one year to realize that this was not a sustainable venture.

I once again gathered up my courage and started a private multidisciplinary practice within an existing practice. A physiotherapy friend, Lyle Hamilton, arranged for us to use the clinic space and equipment in the private physiotherapy practice he managed; it was expected that earnings would go to the practice, while at the same time, pay for our employees. Then I found a dietitian, a nurse and a social worker, and we went to work. It took just a little over a year to realize that although demand was high, a large percentage of clients did not have insurance coverage for cardiac rehabilitation services other than physiotherapy. To make matters worse, a number of health care community members thought we were in it for the money; they were reluctant to support the business by referring patients. In addition, we felt it wise that because we were dealing with a cardiac population, medical input would be invaluable. But paying medical interns and residents $100 an hour to sleep in the back room did not seem to be the best way to accomplish that goal!

It was "back to the drawing board." I teamed up with an amazing registered nurse, Wendy Earle, and together we established a legal, equal, general partnership. Then we had to find the start-up funding - lots of "love money" and personal savings. Next we found another dietitian and a psychologist, and all four of us began to work "pro bono" to get our business up and running. We sought medical help and found two cardiologists, Dr. Gary Burgraff and Dr. Tony Sanfilippo, with hearts of gold and a lot of good advice. This crew eventually developed a landlord-tenant relationship with a local ambulatory care hospital, which allowed us to be closer to emergency services. Soon we were paying our staff. It was a great accomplishment, and we all loved the clients and the metamorphoses they went through during rehabilitation.

While all of this was happening, I was employed by Queen's University as an adjunct faculty member, which grew into a full-time associate professorship; Wendy was offered a nursing position at the local tertiary care hospital that she couldn't refuse; and the Ministry of Health was contemplating funding cardiac rehabilitation services in the province of Ontario. In the late 90s, now the sole proprietor of The Community Cardiac Rehabilitation Centre, I approached the three CEOs of the local hospitals and offered them the business. All three accepted and took on the service jointly. The Cardiac Rehabilitation Centre is now a full-time ambulatory care service. In 2000, it started receiving temporary Ministry funding, and as of 2006 it is under annual, permanent funding through the hospitals' global budgets.

As a result of these experiences, and in my position as a faculty member in a rehabilitation education program, I realized that we were doing a disservice to rehabilitation students if we did not teach business in the professional programs across the country. Still naïve in the ways of the world (this time academia), I pitched the idea of a business course to the head of the Physical Therapy Program, thinking that the business school faculty might be drawn into the picture. The department agreed that it was a good idea, decided to go forward with the semester course I had proposed, but made it clear that the budget could not be stretched to provide funding to bring in outside instructors at that time. I was back in the position of desperately wanting to move forward but not having the full skillset to do so. Rather than do the smart thing and decline, I once again charged on.

For the last five years, we have had a full-semester course in business in the School of Rehabilitation Therapy at Queen's. Along the way, I dragged Mark Edmonds, a hospital administrator extraordinaire, and Peter Schell, a local entrepreneurship expert, into the course as co-instructors and spreadsheet gurus. With the counsel of the Centre for Enterprise Development at Queen's and many, many business owners and leaders in the province and across the country, we have been able to give the students the building blocks towards private practice ownership and/or business management prior to graduation. In addition, and way back when we began offering the course, I discovered Bradley Roulston, creator and owner of Roulston Financial. I asked him to come and speak to the students regarding personal finances. Not only did he do so, but also he was terrific at it! Brad has been coming, first from Toronto and now from BC, every year to not only address students in the course at Queen's but also at most of the other rehabilitation programs across Canada.

What's been missing is a "non-textbook" of sorts to make the business of private health care practice come to life. So the next step was to compile all the years of instruction and advice into a cohesive whole in a way that was easy to read, non-threatening, and yet realistic. That is the book you have just picked up. I hope it will be a handy resource for anyone who wishes to delve into private practice or who is there now but might like some new insights.

If nothing else, perhaps this will be a fun way to prevent insomnia if you keep it on your bedside table for a little bedtime reading.

Enjoy!

Diana M. Hopkins-Rosseel

Table of Contents

PART III: APPENDICES

PART IV: ENCLOSURES

1.   **Spreadsheet Template – CD-ROM**
2.   **Cost of Goods and Services Spreadsheet Template – CD-ROM**
3.   **Sample Business Plans CD-ROM**

PART I

Starting a Private Practice

DIANA HOPKINS-ROSSEEL

CHAPTER 1
Entrepreneurship: Have *You* Got it in You?

DIANA H. HOPKINS-ROSSEEL,DEC, BSC(PT), MSC(REHAB), MCPA

Picture walking into a roomful of your neighbours and asking the question: "What did you do last weekend?" Ken read a fantasy, Bruce was in a swimming competition, Jian took her children to the climbing gym, Chantal answers "bungee jumping," Lumumba finished building his pottery shed behind the house, Paramjeet went for a motorcycle ride, Conrad studied for his exams, Kieran finished some office work, Jean jogged, and Aruna cleaned her house and paid her bills. Can you pick out the entrepreneurs? Perhaps risk takers Chantal and Paramjeet, or the businessman Kieran, or the competitor Bruce? Is it the risk taking that makes you jump to that conclusion? If so, you may have miscalculated. Read on to see why ...

TAKE HOME MESSAGE

If you have many of the traits and characteristics of an entrepreneur, you have taken your first step towards business success.

Corollary: Beware of the wary.

Of course, it is not as simple as an intuitive stab at the question, but there is some truth in the convention that the majority of individuals who are successful in business have many of the same personality traits. Conversely, a potential investor in your proposed business will run for the door if they don't believe you have the innate characteristics of the quintessential entrepreneur.

The first step in the process of starting a small business is to find out about yourself. Do you fit the personality profile of an entrepreneur? From the following list of the 20 most common traits and characteristics associated with business success, check off all of those that you believe apply to you. The more you possess, the more chances you have of being a successful entrepreneur.

Common Characteristics of Entrepreneurs

☐ Innovative, creative

☐ Patient

☐ Persistent

☐ A leader

☐ Versatile, flexible

☐ Independent, self-reliant

☐ Economically driven

☐ Self-confident

☐ Competitive

☐ Interactive, seek out associations with others

☐ Excellent physical health

☐ Organized

☐ Hard working

☐ A desire to take the initiative

☐ A high energy level

☐ A team player

☐ A strong need to achieve, ambitious

☐ Curious

☐ A tolerance for uncertainty

☐ A "calculated risk" taker

1.1 What is an Entrepreneur?

An entrepreneur is someone who is highly responsive to change, sees opportunities that others may not see, and mobilizes resources to make new things happen. A key factor often cited is the willingness-the drive-to take risks.

In fact, past research has shown that entrepreneurs do not have a great willingness to knowingly take risks. This may sound counter-intuitive; however, what scholars suggest is that it is the perception of risk and its possibility of disappointing outcomes that differ among individuals. Even when evaluating identical situations, some people conclude the situation is very risky, whereas others believe it is not (Nutt, 1993). A study by Simon, Houghton, & Aquino (2000) suggests that risk perceptions may differ because certain types of cognitive biases (common types of mental shortcuts used to make judgments) lead individuals to perceive less risk. Therefore, it is not the level of risk or an individual's willingness to take risks; rather, it is many other personal attributes that motivate you to pursue such an undertaking.

TAKE HOME MESSAGE

80% of women and 78% of men say owning or operating their own business has been a change for the better.

Corollary: Challenges are frequently your best opportunities.

Let's take Chantal, the bungee jumper. To most, this activity seems frivolous. Yet on closer examination, she has chosen an activity with such monumental perceived risk, that the bungee jumping company has put into place numerous levels of safeguards to ensure that the worst never (or almost never) happens. The key question is not only what she risked, but what she stood to gain: the risk/benefit ratio is key. Entrepreneurs risk financial stability and certainty to gain autonomy, personal growth, and, ultimately, potentially significant financial gain. Perhaps Chantal's zest for excitement, paired with the safeguards in place, helped her to conclude that the joy of the jump outweighed the risk of injury.

Although some people feel that entrepreneurs are born, not made, experience has shown us that entrepreneurship can be taught, and that a positive environment encourages entrepreneurial thinking and promotes innovation. You may feel as if you are jumping off a cliff into the unknown, but if you put on your parachute and learn to use it before you jump, odds are you will land safely.

An Entrepreneur

► *sees* an opportunity to take advantage of or a problem that needs solving;

► *adds* energy,
drive,
decisiveness,
adabtability,
perserverance,
intuition,
and a

► *pinch* of social skills;

► *mixes* those attributes with voracious learning of that knowledge or those skills they are lacking; and

► *adds* endless hard work to create success.

1.2 How Do You Know if You Really Have it in You?

Your actions are likely to give you away. Do you see opportunities all around you? Do you wear a t-shirt touting "Everything's Negotiable?" When you fail at something, do you see it as a learning opportunity and keep trying, or do you give up? Do your friends describe you as a problem-solver? Given two options, do you gravitate towards the more challenging of the two? Where are you most likely to get your greatest satisfaction: from setting a goal and achieving it, or from the comfort of a job well done? So, you have the attitude, but do you have the abilities?

In the end, if you believe you have the drive, the only way to know if you have the ability is to take the next step ... seize your idea and run with it!

For more insights into entrepreneurship try the Government of Canada's Business Start-Up Assistant:
http://bsa.canadabusiness.ca/gol/bsa/site.nsf/

For a self-assessment quiz try the Business Development Bank of Canada's Entrepreneurial Self-Assessment:
http://www.bdc.ca/en/business_tools/entrepreneurial_self-Assessment

According to a Canadian Imperial Bank of Commerce (CIBC) report entitled "Start Me Up: A Look at New Entrepreneurs in Canada," (2004) an increasing number of health professionals are running with their business ideas. In fact, one of the fastest growing segments of the newly self-employed are those in the health field. The number of new entrepreneurs in this category had risen by 10% between 2002 and 2004 nationally.

Figure 1.1 Growth in Start-ups by Occupation

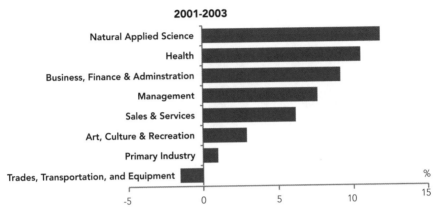

Source: CIBC (2004).

The study suggests that the newer focus on health care is also generating both regular employment (total employment in the sector rose by a strong 175,000) and the creation of start-ups in the industry.

Just one last interesting point to take note of for the entrepreneur who is successful at starting their private practice: there may be a "glitch." The entrepreneur who naturally thrives on the excitement, skill, and hard work that goes into starting a private practice must realize that the characteristics that made them accomplish their goal may not be the characteristics of the person who will run the business well over the long-term …

In Fagenson's (1993) study, entitled *Personal Value Systems Of Men And Women Entrepreneurs Versus Managers*, 255 men and women entrepreneurs and managers rank-ordered 15 terminal (desired end states) and 15 instrumental (methods used by individuals to achieve desired end states) values. The results of the study revealed that the gender of individuals had very little influence on their value systems, while managers and entrepreneurs had vastly different value systems. Whereas managers prefer to enjoy the pleasures that life has to offer, entrepreneurs want to be free to achieve and actualize their potential. Once a business is well underway, managing the operation becomes central to its success. The

TAKE HOME MESSAGE

Continual innovation and review may be the key to longevity for the entrepreneur.

Corollary:
Partners with different values and skills may be just the antidote.

results of the study suggest that this change in role emphasis may not be satisfying to the entrepreneur because the value system of individuals who are committed to the managerial role is at odds with the value preferences of entrepreneurs. This may help explain why many entrepreneurs become less interested and motivated in their ventures once the entrepreneurial component of their job is overtaken by the management component.

REFERENCES

CIBC World Markets Inc. (2004). *Start Me Up: A Look at New Entrpreneurs in Canada.* Economics and Strategy. Retrieved May 28, 2007, from http://research.cibcwm.com/economic_public/download/sup-06172004.pdf.

Fagenson, E. (1993). Personal value systems of men and women entrepreneurs versus managers. *Journal of Business Venturing, 8*(4), 409-430.

Nutt, P.C. (1993). Flexible decision styles and the choices of top executives. *Journal of Management Studies, 30*(5), 695-721.

Simon, M., Houghton, S.M., & Aquino, K. (2000). Cognitive biases, risk perception, and venture formation: How individuals decide to start companies. *Journal of Business Venturing, 15*(2), (March), 113-134.

ADDITIONAL READING

Brockhaus, R.H., Sr. (1980). Risk-taking propensity of entrepreneurs. *Academy of Management Journal, 23*(3), 509–520.

Kahneman, D., & Lovallo, D. (1993). Timid choices and bold forecasts: A cognitive perspective on risk-taking. *Management Science, 39*(1), 17–31.

MacCrimmon, K.R., & Wehrung, D.A. (1990). Characteristics of risk-taking executives. *Management Science, 36*(4), 422–435.

March, J., & Shapira, Z. (1987). Managerial perspective on risk and risk-taking. *Management Science, 3,* 1404–1418.

CHAPTER 2
The Health Care Environment
MICHEL D. LANDRY, PT, PhD

Consider this weighty chapter as a rite of passage. It may help you to imagine a lofty and personal scenario! In this chapter, you will learn about the core elements of the Canadian health care system and rehabilitation industry, and discover how population statistics can be made to work for you.

Picture yourself surveying this beautiful country from the top of the Peace Tower on Parliament Hill. Somewhere out there you are planning to set up your very own business. But just what environment will your business encounter "out there?" One of the first important steps you can take on this journey is to understand the very foundation upon which you are standing. Gain a strong competitive edge and read this chapter until both the landscape and the environment feel familiar.

Knowing the Basics: Your Competitive Advantage

Access to publicly-funded health care is a defining element of the Canadian identity. The rehabilitation industry however, represents a clear departure from this single-payer, publicly-funded system. As a result, before thinking about going into business, you'll need to understand the basic structure and changing landscape of the Canadian health care system. Knowing the basics represents a competitive advantage; consequently, the entrepreneur can position their business ideas and solutions within a "bigger picture." As health care continues to change, this knowledge will provide the context for you to implement your business strategy in a way to take full advantage of these changes.

2.1 The Canadian Health Care System: Public "Crisis" versus Private Opportunity

Canada's national health system, also known as Medicare (not to be confused with the American Medicare system), was crafted to ensure that medically necessary hospital and physician services would be available to Canadians based on their need, not their ability to pay. Indeed, since its inception in the 1960s, the national health care system has become a beacon of the Canadian commitment to social egalitarian values. However, more than 40 years later, there are increasing financial pressures and conceptual challenges facing Medicare. The result has been a lingering sense of "crisis," stimulating the production of multiple health policy reports (e.g., the Kirby Report [2002] and the Romanow Report [2002]) concerning the status of the country's health system.

Much of the rhetoric around the crisis in health care focuses on 1984 – the year the *Canada Health Act* (CHA) received Royal Assent. The Act has become a paradox in the health care environment: some perceive it as a "protector" of the nation's single-payer, publicly-funded health care system; and yet at the same time, others view it as an institutional barrier to developing a more progressive health care system that meets the current needs of Canadians. As might be predicted, stakeholders and pressure groups use the language of the Act, and their perception of its intent, to defend their particular interests. The CHA was enshrined by the federal government as a means of protecting Canadians from extra-billing; additionally, it defined the terms and conditions of a publicly "insured" service across all provinces and territories. Table 2.1 highlights the Act's five guiding principles for insurable services within Medicare.

The "comprehensiveness" principle is the most misunderstood, widely quoted, and intensely debated of the five principles. To some degree, this condition was based on previous legislation and effectively defined an insured service in terms of who delivers it and where it is delivered. In this case, the "who" implies physicians, and the "where" implies hospitals. Under the CHA's rules and regulations, provinces and territories can, but are not legally forced to, insure care beyond these institutional boundaries.

Table 2.1 The Five Principles of the *Canada Health Act*

Public Administration:	Provincial and territorial health care insurance plans must be administered and operated on a non-profit basis by a public authority, accountable to the provincial or territorial government.
Comprehensiveness:	The comprehensiveness criterion of the *Canada Health Act* requires that, in order to be eligible for federal cash transfer payments, the health care insurance plan of a province or territory "must insure all insured health services provided by hospital, medical practitioners or dentists (i.e., surgical-dental services which require a hospital setting).
Universality:	All insured residents of a province or territory must be entitled to the insured health services provided by the provincial or territorial health care insurance plan on uniform terms and conditions.
Portability:	Residents moving from one province or territory to another must continue to be covered for insured health care services by the "home" jurisdiction during any waiting period imposed by the new province or territory of residence.
Accessibility:	Residents of a province or territory must have reasonable access to insured hospital, medical, and surgical-dental services on uniform terms and conditions.

Note. Adapted from Health Canada (2005)

2.1.1 What about Rehabilitation?

Regarding rehabilitation services, physiotherapy is the only service that is explicitly mentioned under the "hospital services" condition in the CHA (see Table 2.2).

Based on this provision, it would appear that there should be little or no debate on whether physiotherapy services are insured under the Act. However, upon closer interpretation, it is not as clear as one might expect, and as the saying goes, "the devil is in the detail." More precisely, section (h) of the hospital condition reads: "use of physiotherapy facilities." This is vague terminology use and does little to indicate the level of access to the service. The term "use" does not indicate or imply that the provision is guaranteed; it simply indicates that should facilities be accessible and available, they may be used for the purposes of physiotherapy services. The term "physiotherapy," is a non-specified designation that is not yet reserved to any one group of regulated professionals (although the terms "physiotherapist" and "physical therapist" are indeed restricted).

Table 2.2 The *Canada Health Act*'s Statement on Physical Therapy

> **"Hospital services" refers to any of the following services provided to in-patients or out-patients at a hospital, if the services are medically necessary for the purpose of maintaining health, preventing disease or diagnosing or treating an injury, illness, or disability, namely,**
>
> (a) accommodation and meals at the standard or public ward level and preferred accommodation if medically required,
>
> (b) nursing service,
>
> (c) laboratory, radiological, and other diagnostic procedures, together with the necessary interpretations,
>
> (d) drugs, biologicals, and related preparations when administered in the hospital,
>
> (e) use of operating room, case room, and anaesthetic facilities, including necessary equipment and supplies,
>
> (f) medical and surgical equipment and supplies,
>
> (g use of radiotherapy facilities,
>
> **(h) use of physiotherapy facilities, and (emphasis added)**
>
> (i) services provided by persons who receive remuneration therefore from the hospital, but does not include services that are excluded by the regulations.

Note. Adapted from Health Canada (1985)

It would therefore appear that, although the word "physiotherapy" is used, physiotherapy services might face interpretation issues within the Act. The wording of the Act may not be specific enough to protect physiotherapy services from legislative challenges; and although it may not have been the original intent, the legislation can exclude physiotherapy-especially outpatient and ambulatory community services-from hospital services. This lack of precision also affects other rehabilitation services.

Rehabilitation practitioners across Canada may believe-and assume-that their services are medically necessary to the health of Canadians, while other stakeholders may not necessarily share this view. As a result, outpatient and ambulatory rehabilitation services are increasingly being funded through private sources, and delivered through a mix of small and large for-profit providers. It is this shift out of the public domain that has spawned the increased role of private institutions in both the funding and delivery of health and rehabilitation services.

2.1.2 Public and Private Sector Trends

Remember your view from the Peace Tower: you can see people and resources travelling in many directions. The same is true for health care funding. Read on to discover how trends in our system are impacting the flow of funds being spent on health care.

What does a shift from public to private or a combination of the two, really mean to the private rehabilitation entrepreneur? Well, let's start by recognizing that the term "public/private mix" refers to the precarious balance that exists between the public and private sectors in the funding and/or delivery of services. The term "public" refers to a variety of definitions ranging from government to semi-autonomous agencies. Similarly, the term "private" can also refer to a variety of definitions ranging from not-for-profit and charitable agencies to for-profit corporations. Table 2.3 outlines the distinctions between public and private.

Table 2.3 Categories of Public and Private Institutions

▼ Public	▼ Private
• Federal (national government)	• Private not-for-profit
• Sub-national (province/territory government)	• Private for-profit small business
• Regional government/authorities	• Private for-profit corporations
• Local government	• Individuals and families

It is important to note that the terms "public" and "private" are not always used with a great deal of precision. For instance, hospitals in Ontario are often called "public" hospitals because they are legislated under the Government of Ontario's *Public Hospital Act* (1990). However, these hospitals are not generally publicly owned; in fact, 98% are owned and operated by private, not-for-profit charitable institutions (Taylor, 2002). Referring to hospitals as "public" may not be as accurate as calling them "private" institutions that are funded primarily through "public" means. This ambiguity in the definitions of public and private occurs in the funding, delivery, and allocation dimensions.

2.1.3 Funding, Delivery, and Allocation

Health systems include three primary dimensions: (1) funding (how services are paid or funded); (2) delivery (organizational structure of the provider); and (3) allocation (the way in which financing is transferred from payer to service provider).

2.1.3.1 Funding

There is a broad range of public and private funding arrangements for health care services. At the same time, depending on the expenditure category, there is a wide variation in the proportion of public/private funding. For example, it is generally accepted that the total public/private mix of Canadian health care funding is a 70/30 split: 70% of funding is obtained through public means, 30% is obtained through various types of private funding. Figure 2.1 shows the percentage of public and private funding for the eight expenditure categories of the Canadian Institute for Health Information (CIHI).

Figure 2.1 Public/Private Shares of Total Health Expenditures per the Expenditure Categories of the Canadian Institute for Health Information (CIHI) (2001)

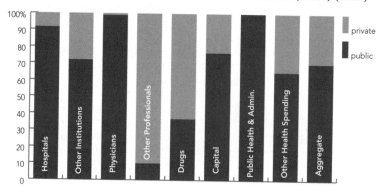

Note. Adapted from Canadian Institute for Health Information (2001)

Although the total (aggregate) indicates that 70% of overall health expenditures are derived from the public sector, this is not necessarily the case within each individual expenditure category. For instance, approximately 92% of "hospital" expenditures are derived from public sources whereas in the "other professional" category (including rehabilitation services delivered outside of hospitals), only 10% of expenditures are derived from public sources. Thus, there are significant differences between the public and private share of financing services across different expenditure categories. More specifically, there are three primary categories of funding within the rehabilitation sector types (see Table 2.4).

It may be interesting to note that there is some indication that the "public" category is diminishing in terms of total expenditures and unit price while generally, the "quasi-public" and "private" categories appear to be increasing. In other words, while the public funding category is shrinking, the other categories are expanding. This trend may represent the ideal policy shift for the entrepreneur;

however it must be cautioned that these expanding funding categories (i.e., private casualty insurers) are doing so reluctantly; consequently, they are attempting to contain their increasing costs.

Table 2.4 Funding Categories for Rehabilitation

Funding Categories	Description	Examples
▸ Public	Public sources of funding refer to financing that is derived from federal, provincial/territorial, and/or municipal governments.	• Hospitals • Long-term care facilities • Community Care Access Centres (home care) • Veterans Affairs Canada
▸ Quasi-Public	Quasi-public sources of funding refer to programs that are funded through private sources, but where the fee structure is regulated in some form by the provincial government.	• Motor Vehicle Accident (MVA) insurance • Workers' Compensation
▸ Private	Private sources refer to financial sources that are derived purely from private sources and are under no government control.	• Private casualty insurance (extended health benefits) • Out-of-pocket payments

Note: Often, only regulated rehabilitation practitioners are able to receive payment within public and quasi-public payers; however, these restrictions are less important to private payers. (Please refer to individual payer streams to determine the extent to which regulated and non-regulated practitioners are eligible.)

2.1.3.2 Delivery

The second dimension of health systems is their delivery. Individual practitioners generally work within some type of provider organization (i.e., hospitals, home care agencies, private for-profit firms). In rehabilitation, the primary practitioners can be categorized into three types (see Table 2.5).

Table 2.5 Rehabilitation Provider Types

Provider Types	Description	Examples
▸ Public	Public ownership of the facility by the federal, provincial/territorial, or municipal governments.	• Psychiatric hospitals • Military hospitals • A few community hospitals
▸ Private Not-For-Profit	Facility is privately owned, but operated on a cost recovery basis.	• Majority of hospitals • Institutions • Community organizations
▸ Private For-Profit	The operation has a goal and expectation to generate profits in the delivery of services.	• Privately-owned clinics • Corporately-owned network of clinics

If you are considering going into business for yourself or with others, you will likely be considering a private for-profit business structure. It is essential that you understand where your business will be positioned within the larger context. You must also be aware of the growth of the for-profit sector in the last decade, as it is an indication of the shift to private markets. However, the majority of these private ventures are "general" in that they service a wide client base with many clinical conditions and funding types. The successful proprietor will be willing to adapt their services and products to accommodate changes in clientele and funding needs. This may mean moving to and from niche and general practice models.

2.1.3.3 Allocation

The third and last dimension that defines a health care system is allocation: the incentive structures set up to distribute funds from payer to provider of services. In rehabilitation there are a multitude of allocation methods, ranging from fee-for-service (FFS) to program fees within a particular institution. In a FFS model, the provider invoices the payer for each unit of service or each visit, whereas a program fee would include an envelope of funding for clients who fit a specific clinical profile (e.g., minor soft tissue whiplash without neurological signs). Each funding type has various methods of payment distribution to the provider, and as such it is important for any new enterprise to determine and explore these methods.

Each of these different methods may have specific unit prices. It falls to the independent business owner to understand these mechanisms in order to determine the extent to which a profit potential exists: there must be sufficient monies coming

in to offset the costs of operation. For instance, in Ontario (as of the writing of this chapter), the unit price for injured workers (funded through the Workplace Safety & Insurance Board [WSIB]) is $18.41 per visit. Many practitioners have determined that this price is lower than their costs of operation and have made a business decision to no longer accept WSIB clients in their clinics. This decision is legal, as long as the provider does not treat any WSIB clients. If the provider "picks and chooses" WSIB clients, it can be seen as a violation of regulatory college standards of practice (see Saltman & von Otter, 1992; Hollander, Deber, & Jacobs, 1998; Saltman & Figueras, 1998, for further details regarding the allocation dimension and the incentive that underpins each model). It is important to note that payers of rehabilitation are rapidly moving away from FFS models in favour of the program fee as a way to contain and predict costs.

2.2 The Outlook in the Rehabilitation Industry: Putting Statistics to Work for You

There are many variables that contribute to a positive outlook in the rehabilitation industry. This section will focus on population growth as an indicator, with only minor commentary of other equally important variables such as mortality, morbidity, and disability rates.

Your bird's eye view from the Peace Tower gives you a fabulous opportunity to see the population as a whole and with the added benefits of the statistics offered in this chapter, you can put these selective facts to work for you as you plan your business.

2.2.1 A Positive Outlook!
The Canadian population has maintained a positive growth pattern since 2001 (see Table 2.6). Although the country's population as a whole continues to grow, this is not the case in all provinces/territories. For instance, Newfoundland and Labrador demonstrated negative population growth rates between 2001 and 2004, whereas Saskatchewan only recently reported a modest 0.1% growth rate between 2003 and 2004. All other jurisdictions had positive growth rates during this period, including Ontario with a growth rate that surpassed the national rate. Population growth is an important variable to consider for the entrepreneur who plans to develop a business venture in an area that has a large population base, or where a population base is expected to grow in the future. (You can search www.statscan.ca for the most recent statistics regarding population growth in your area.)

TAKE HOME MESSAGE

Just as in Real Estate: location, location, location.

Corollary: Location, location, location!

Table 2.6 Population Growth in Canada 2001–2005

LOCATION	YEAR					GROWTH RATE (%)			
	2001	2002	2003	2004	2005	01-02	02-03	03-04	04-05
Canada	31,021,251	31,372,587	31,660,466	31,946,316	32,378,122	1.10	0.90	0.90	1.30
Newfoundland and Labrador	521,986	519,449	518,350	517,027	515,591	-0.50	-0.20	-0.30	-0.20
Prince Edward Island	136,672	136,934	137,266	137,864	138,278	0.20	0.20	0.40	0.30
Nova Scotia	932,389	934,507	936,165	936,960	938,116	0.20	0.20	0.10	0.10
New Brunswick	749,890	750,327	750,896	751,384	751,726	0.10	0.10	0.10	0.04
Quebec	7,396,990	7,445,754	7,492,333	7,542,760	7,616,645	0.70	0.60	0.70	1.00
Ontario	11,897,647	12,102,045	12,256,645	12,392,721	12,589,823	1.70	1.30	1.10	1.60
Manitoba	1,151,285	1,155,584	1,161,552	1,170,268	1,178,109	0.40	0.50	0.70	0.70
Saskatchewan	1,000,134	995,886	994,428	995,391	992,995	-0.40	-0.10	0.10	-0.30
Alberta	3,056,739	3,116,332	3,158,641	3,201,895	3,281,296	1.90	1.30	1.40	2.50
British Columbia	4,078,447	4,115,413	4,152,289	4,196,383	4,271,210	0.90	0.90	1.10	1.80
Yukon	30,129	30,137	30,554	31,209	31,235	0.00	1.40	2.10	0.10
Northwest Territories	40,822	41,489	42,206	42,810	42,965	1.60	1.70	1.40	0.40
Nunavut	28,121	28,739	29,141	29,644	30,133	2.20	1.40	1.70	1.70

Note. Adapted from Statistics Canada (2007)

2.2.2 There's More to Life...

Statistics Canada (2005) reported that life expectancy rates have also increased for all Canadians. Life expectancy (if born in 2002) reached 77.2 years for males and 82.1 years for females; the combined life expectancy for both males and females was 79.7 years, indicating a 1.4-year increase from 1996. A trend that is particularly important is that life expectancy is rising among seniors as compared to previous generations. There were 3.92 million Canadians 65+ in 2001; this number is expected to swell to 6.7 million in 2021 (Health Canada, 2005). By 2041, 1 in 4 Canadians will be in this group, a total of 9.2 million people. The reasons given for longer life expectancy include a variety of factors ranging from the environment to nutrition. From a health delivery perspective, it is clear that increasingly effective interventions (medical and rehabilitative) have also contributed to longer life expectancies. At the same time, there are significant concerns regarding trends such as childhood and adolescent obesity, lower levels of physical activity, and increased risk-taking behaviours that could, in the near future, affect these rates.

Life expectancy at birth is rising in Canada for both males and females; however, as one grows older the relative risk of developing and/or acquiring a disability also increases. Population data from 1996 indicates that, although life expectancy at birth may be increasing, so are the years spent with a disability. In other words, even though the national life expectancy in 1996 was 78.3 years, 12.4% (or 9.7 years) of an average Canadian's life will be spent living with some form of disability (Statistics Canada, 2001a).

2.2.3 Statistics and Disability

In 2001, 3.6 million Canadians living in households reported having an activity restriction (disability) representing a disability rate of 12.4% (Table 2.7).

The data show that although Canadians are growing older, they are also increasing their probability of developing and living with a disability. Furthermore, disability rates gradually increase with age starting with a 3.3% disability rate among children aged 0–14 years. This proportion rises to 10% among adults aged 15–64 years. By the age of 65, the rate of disability is 40%, and Statistics Canada (2001b) reports that 53.3% of persons 75+ report living with a disability. From a population health perspective, it is expected that the absolute number of persons with disabilities will increase dramatically along with population growth; consequently, as they grow older, Canadians will likely have increased health and rehabilitation needs. The *Profile of Disability Report* (2001a) published by Statistics Canada indicates that the cost of short-term disability is $9.8 billion per year, and long-term disability $32.2 billion per year. In particular there is growing concern that "baby boomers" (defined as those Canadians born between 1946–1964) is in decline, and that this cohort will ultimately

TAKE HOME MESSAGE

There is an emerging trend of shifting care to the community, closer to where the client and their family lives. This shift also transitions the system from public to private payment.

Corollary: There are opportunities for private rehabilitations enterprises.

increase demand on the health system. The indirect costs (i.e., time lost due to long- and short-term disabilities), and the value of future productivity lost due to premature mortality and morbidity in Canada represents an estimated economic value of $129 billion, nearly 21% of the Gross Domestic Product (GDP) (the annual total value of goods produced and services provided in a country, excluding transactions with other countries) (Public Health Agency of Canada, 1998).

Table 2.7 Population with Disabilities and Disability Rates (2001)

	Total Population	Population without Disabilities	Population with Disabilities	Percentage Of Population with Disabilities (%)
Canada	28,991,770	25,390,510	3,601,270	12.4
Newfoundland and Labrador	492,800	432,310	60,500	12.3
Prince Edward Island	132,850	113,880	18,970	14.3
Nova Scotia	888,000	736,690	152,210	17.1
New Brunswick	712,300	609,440	102,860	14.4
Quebec	7,052,790	6,457,100	595,690	8.4
Ontario	11,192,730	9,678,350	1,514,380	13.5
Manitoba	1,036,270	888,690	147,580	14.2
Saskatchewan	859,080	734,870	124,210	14.5
Alberta	2,830,280	2,475,540	354,740	12.5
British Columbia	3,793,770	3,263,640	530,130	14.0

Note. Adapted from Statistics Canada, (2001b)
Data excludes Yukon, Northwest Territories, and Nunavut.

The aging population is not the only driver in the rehabilitation industry. Advancements in acute medical care have improved mortality rates following illness, disease, and trauma. All of these create increased demand for other services – such as rehabilitation – that can and will improve the functional capacity of affected individuals. Thus, it becomes evident that the combination of longer life spans, and decreasing rates of mortality and morbidity will have serious effects on the health care system. The number of new cases in stroke, spinal cord injury, musculoskeletal injuries, and other categories are increasing, thereby creating an expanding market for rehabilitation services.

2.3 Projections on the Future Demand for Rehabilitation

No, you don't have crystal ball, but what a clear view from high above the city! With the facts you have just read, the horizon becomes more focused. Use this view to create a business plan in line with the future of the Canadian health care landscape.

Based on what is already known regarding population growth and support for community-based rehabilitation services, the needs for such services are expected to grow at least for the next two decades. The drivers of this trend also include improved survival rates following illness, disease and trauma, and the emergence of priorities such as the prevention and expansion of the continuum of care. Combining these trends with the predictions made in *The Sustainability Report* (Institute for Research and Innovation in Sustainability, 2003), there will be a population growth of 14% between 2001 and 2021. It might be conservatively argued that the number of Canadians affected by clinical pathologies will increase by at least 14%. It is important to note that this 14% increase is a conservative estimate because it does not account for the changing proportions within the overall population growth. As noted previously, the fastest growing cohort of the population are those aged 65+ who are projected to account for 20% of the population in 2021 and 25% in 2041. As this group grows older, its members will require increased rehabilitation services to maintain their function, mobility, and independence. Although there has not been sufficient research conducted in this area, what we presently know can help us predict with certainly that future rehabilitation needs will increase significantly in the next 20 years.

If one accepts that rehabilitation needs will increase, the next important issue to address is to determine whether or not there are sufficient financial and human resources available to offset supply with demand. Although not directly addressed in this chapter, the financial resources of individuals are a key variable in accessing rehabilitation services – that is, even if there is an increasing demand for services, this alone does not signal an expanding market because it is not clear how and who will pay for services. For example, it is a well-known fact that many Canadians "need" a hip or knee replacement; however, due to scarce resources they are unable to access these medically- necessary services, or they may not have the disposable income to pay out-of-pocket costs for these services.

TAKE HOME MESSAGE

The entrepreneur who demonstrates business acumen will be well positioned to use health care funding and delivery changes as commercial opportunities which, in turn, can be translated into healthy financial sustainability.

Corollary: A strong private sector provides necessary rehabilitation services to Canadians

In the end, we recommend that those contemplating a business in clinical practice develop a competitive edge, and remember to make use of trends and updated statistical data. The additional reading list concluding this chapter can help you when planning for your business.

REFERENCES

Canadian Institute for Health Information. (2001). *Health care in Canada – 2001.* Retrieved June 1, 2007, from http://www.cihi.ca

Government of Ontario. (1990). *Public Hospital Act.* Retrieved June 8, 2007, from http://www.e-laws.gov.on.ca/DBLaws/Statutes/English/90p40_e.htm

Health Canada. (1985). *The Canada Health Act.* Retrieved June 8, 2007, from http://laws.justice.gc.ca/en/showdoc/cs/C-6///en?page=1.

Health Canada. (2005). *Canada's Health Care System (Medicare).* Retrieved June 8, 2007, from http://www.hc-sc.gc.ca/hcs-sss/medi-assur/overview-apercu/index_e.html

Health Canada, Division on Aging and Seniors. (2002). *Canada's aging population.* Retrieved June 7, 2007, from http://www.phac-aspc.gc.ca/seniors-aines/pubs/fed_paper/index_e.htm

Hollander, M.J., Deber, R.B., & Jacobs, P., eds. (1998). *A critical review of models of resource allocation and reimbursement in health care: A report prepared for the Ontario Ministry of Health.* Victoria, BC: Canadian Policy Research Networks, Inc.

Institute for Research and Innovation in Sustainability. (2003). *The sustainability report.* Toronto, ON: York University and IRIS.

Kirby, B. (2002). *The health of Canadians: The Federal Role: Volume Six: Recommendations for reform.* The Standing Senate Committee on Social Affairs Science and Technology. Retrieved June 8, 2007, from http://www.parl.gc.ca/37/2/parlbus/commbus/senate/Com-e/soci-e/rep-e/repoct02vol6-e.htm.

Public Health Agency of Canada. (1998). *Economic burden of illness in Canada, 1998.* Retrieved June 7, 2007, from http://www.phac-aspc.gc.ca/publicat/ebic-femc98/.

Romanow, R. J. (2002). *Building on values: The future of health care in Canada: Final report.* Ottawa, ON: Commission on the Future of Health Care in Canada.

Saltman, R.B., & Figueras, J. (1998). Analyzing the evidence on European health care reforms. *Health Affairs, 17*(2), 85–108.

Saltman, R.B. & von Otter, C. (1992). *Planned markets and public competition: Strategic reform in Northern European health systems.* Philadelphia: Open University Press.

Statistics Canada.(2001a). *A profile of disability in Canada, 2001.* Retrieved June 7, 2007, from http://www.statcan.ca/bsolc/english/bsolc?catno=89-577-XIE#formatdisp.

Statistics Canada. (2001b). *Participation and activity limitation survey.* Retrieved June 8, 2007, from http://www.statcan.ca/cgi-bin/imdb/p2SV.pl?Function=getSurvey&SDDS=3251&lang=en&db=IMDB&dbg=f&adm=8&dis=2.

Statistics Canada. (2005). Life expectancy. *Canada Health Report, Vol 17,* No. 1. Retrieved June 8, 2007, from http://www.statcan.ca/bsolc/engligh/bsolc?catno=82-003-X20050018709.

Statistics Canada. (2007). *Canada's population estimates.* Retrieved June 8, 2007, from http://www.statcan.ca/Daily/English/070329/d070329b.htm

Taylor, D.H., Jr. (2002). What price for-profit hospitals? *CMAJ, 166* (11), 1418–1419.

ADDITIONAL READING

Angus, D.E., Auer, L., Cloutier, J.E., & Albert, T. (1995). *Sustainable health care for Canada. Ottawa,* ON: Queen's–University of Ottawa Economic Projects.

Brooks, S. (2000). *Canadian democracy: An introduction.* Don Mills, ON: Oxford University Press.

Deber, R.B. (2000). Getting what we pay for: Myths and realities about financing Canada's health care system. *Health Law in Canada, 21*(2), 9–59.

Deber, R.B. (2002). *Delivering health care services: Public, not-for-profit, or private?* Discussion Paper No. 17, The Commission on the Future of Health Care in Canada, (August). Retrieved June 1, 2007, from http://www.hc-sc.gc.ca/english/care/romanow/hcc0494.html.

Devereaux, P.J., Choi, P.T.L., Lacchetti, C., et al. (2002). A systematic review and meta-analysis of studies comparing mortality rates of private for-profit and private not-for-profit hospitals. *CMAJ, 166* (11), 1399–1406.

Gibson, B., Cott, C., Jaglal, S., & Badley, E. (2001). *Exploring rehabilitation mental health.* Hospital Report 2001, Preliminary Studies Volume One. Retrieved June 8, 2007, from http://www.hospitalreport.ca/2001prelim_vol1.htm

Health Services Restructuring Commission (HSRC) (1998). *Change and transition: planning guidelines and implementation strategies for home care, long term care, mental health, rehabilitation and sub-acute care.* Toronto, ON: Health Services Restructuring Commission).

Hutchison, B., Abelson, J., & Lavis, J. (2001). Primary care in Canada: So much innovation, so little change. *Health Affairs, 20*(3), 116–131.

Landry, M.D. (2004). *Physical Therapy Services in Ontario: Assessing a changing public/private Mix.* Unpublished PhD thesis, Department of Health Policy, Management and Evaluation (HPME), Faculty of Medicine, University of Toronto.

Maioni, A. (1998). *Parting at the crossroads: The emergence of health insurance in the United States and Canada.* Princeton, NJ: Princeton University Press.

Mendelsohn, M. (2002). *Canadians' thoughts on their health care system: Preserving the Canadian model through innovation.* The Commission on the Future of Health Care in Canada, (August). Retrieved June 8, 2007, from http://www.hc-sc.gc.ca/english/care/romanow/hcc0038.html.

Naylor, C.D. (1986). *Private practice, public payment: Canadian medicine and the politics of health insurance 1911-1966.* Montreal/Kingston: McGill-Queens University Press.

Ontario Physiotherapy Association (2000). *Private clinics in public hospital: A discussion paper.* Retrieved July 1, 2005, from http://www.opa.on.ca/.

Rachlis, M. & Kushner, C. (1994). *Strong medicine: How to save Canada's health care system.* Toronto, ON: Harper Collins Publishers Ltd.

Taylor, M.G. (1987). *Health insurance and Canadian public policy.* 2d Ed. Montreal/Kingston: McGill-Queen's University Press.

CHAPTER 3
Your Practice Options
DIANA H. HOPKINS-ROSSEEL,DEC, BSC(PT), MSC(REHAB), MCPA

Sofie is working as an occupational therapist for the local tertiary care hospital but has decided she needs to "get out from under." For months she has been frustrated by the constraints of global budget funding and troubled by her institutional scope of practice. She has decided to open a private practice offering occupational therapy, physiotherapy, speech pathology, social work, and nutritional services for the under-serviced population of individuals with neuromuscular deficits.

Businesses are generally considered a legal entity. Each type of business is governed under different laws and taxed according to different rules. In clinical practice, there are three primary legal business designations: a proprietorship, a partnership, and/or a corporation. What type of business should Sofie develop?

3.1 How about a Sole Proprietorship?

A sole proprietorship is a business owned and operated by one individual. The owner has full control of the assets of the business and is responsible for any business debts. You shouldn't assume however, that establishing a sole proprietorship can be done without the input of a lawyer. At a minimum, it is likely to require the registering and purchasing of licenses and permits both for its operation and for the business name. A quick call to a lawyer in your jurisdiction or to the local economic development agency will get you answers as to what is required, and where to go to complete the registration and/or purchase the license(s). The call to a lawyer may be an initial free consultation or may be at a cost to you; either way it is important to know what you are getting yourself into. A common way to start up a business is to establish yourself as a sole proprietor but with associates (see Chapter 11 for more information on associates), in order to reduce some of the overhead costs such as location, staff, etc. In the case of a sole proprietorship, the profit is taxed on the owner's personal tax return.

3.2 Perhaps a Partnership?

A partnership is "an association or relationship between two or more individuals or corporations that join together to operate a trade or business for profit" (Canadian Bankers Association, 2004, p. 10). A partnership is a legal entity in which legal rights and responsibilities are constitutionally defined (e.g., signing contracts and borrowing money). In the case of a partnership, the business name must be registered. The partnership does not pay income tax but the income generated is reported on the income tax return of each partner. A partnership of six or more persons is required to file federal income tax information forms. It receives a "partnership identification number" from the Canada Revenue Agency.

Partnerships may be either *general* or *limited*. In a *general partnership*, the partners share full ownership of the business assets, assume full responsibility for its debts, and share equal responsibility for running the business. In a *limited partnership*, the general partner (or partners) have unlimited liability for the debts and run the business, while the limited partner (or partners) provide capital and share in the profits or losses of the business. Limited partners are not liable for partnership debts and do not take a hand in running the business. **All partners should ensure they negotiate and sign a written partnership agreement outlining in full, each partner's rights, responsibilities, and obligations.**

Therefore, the advantages and disadvantages of partnerships are arguably the opposite of those of sole proprietorship: there is a loss of independence and control, however, sharing in the financial, legal, and managerial responsibilities of the business may outweigh this reduction in autonomy.

3.3 Maybe Incorporation is the Answer?

You may be authorized by law to form a separate legal entity known as a corporation. The best way to understand a corporation is to think of it as an individual: the corporation has all the legal rights of an individual and is responsible for its own debts. The distinction is that the owners or shareholders are protected from the corporation's liabilities. If a corporation goes bankrupt, only the assets of the business may go to pay off its creditors. If an unincorporated business goes into bankruptcy, not only are the business assets used to pay off the debts, but also the owner's personal assets can be sought out and seized. This puts the owner's home and belongings at great risk. Under Canadian law, there are many tax benefits to incorporating.

In Canada, the jurisdictions for incorporation are provincial/territorial. Therefore, before making the decision to incorporate you should seek the advice of a lawyer to help you navigate the process. In addition, there are limitations in many jurisdictions on health professionals incorporating their practices. This may have a bearing not only on whether you incorporate, but also who the owners or shareholders will be. A professional corporation resembles a business corporation, requiring compliance with corporate law, but it must also follow the rules and regulations of the relevant professional regulatory agency (or agencies). A professional corporation is formed in the same manner as a business corporation, except that it typically has one or more additional limitations, depending on the jurisdiction. For example, professional corporations are typically required to use the name of the professional as part of the corporate name. They may also have to include the words "Professional Corporation" as part of their legal name.

Moreover, the professional corporation may be required to obtain a certificate of registration from the professional regulatory agency so as to ensure that no disciplinary action is pending before the professional association against any of the licensed directors, shareholders, or employees of the corporation. As a health care professional, your regulatory body will provide you with guidance on the regulatory aspects of incorporation.

3.4 Making The Choice Clearer

Sofie needs to look at the pros and cons of each type of business, along with her personal aspirations and abilities in light of her particular proposed business venture. Let's compare ...

Table 3.1 Pros and Cons of each Business Type

Attribute	Sole Proprietorship	Partnership	Incorporation
Control	Total	Shared	Shared by general partners
Defined legal rights and responsibilities	⌀	✓	✓✓
Tax advantages	⌀	⌀	✓✓
Financial risk	Total	Shared by general partners	Shared by owners
Administrative and management workload	Total	Shared by general partners (including personal assets)	Shared by owners (only the assets of the business)
Liability protection	⌀	⌀	✓✓
Cost of registration	(↑)	↑	↑↑
Contract costs	(↑)	↑	↑↑

Legend: ⌀   *Does not apply to the attribute*
       ✓   *Applies to the attribute*
     ✓✓   *Does apply and has the potential for significant advantage*
   (↑)   *There may be a cost associated depending on the jurisdiction or the negotiation*
     ↑   *There is a nominal cost/fee attached*
    ↑↑   *There is a significant cost/fee attached*

It seems that the balance of the decision rests on how Sofie weighs the benefits of complete autonomy and profit, compared to those of shared risk and workload. If she wants complete autonomy and profits, she should go for the sole proprietorship. If, on the other hand, she would like to spread the work and limit her financial investment, a partnership appears to be the best option. With such an ambitious and highly risky financial business such as a multidisciplinary practice, Sofie would be wise to lean towards the partnership. If you add her lack of private practice experience to the equation, she should perhaps be looking for a partner with business ownership and/or management experience.

TAKE HOME MESSAGE

Your choice of legal business ownership type reflects both your management style and your financial risk profile.

Corollary: Put it in writing

Although the decision to incorporate can be costly, there is greater protection of both the corporation and its owners. Considering the relatively unproven territory of private services for individuals with neurological deficits, and taking into account the size of a large multidisciplinary venture, in the end, Sofie chose to incorporate her clinic, limiting the risk to her personal assets, and allowing her to learn in a less risky and more supportive environment.

It is now time to formulate a plan and answer the timeless questions of:

Who?

What?

Where?

When?

Why?

and How?

REFERENCE

Canadian Banker's Association. 3rd Ed. (October 2004). *Getting Started in Small Business* (Small Business Services, Tools and Resources). Retrieved April 29, 2007, from: http://www.cba.ca/.

CHAPTER 4
The Business Plan: From Beginning to End
DIANA H. HOPKINS-ROSSEEL,DEC, BSC(PT), MSC(REHAB), MCPA

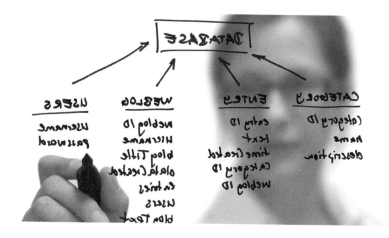

A loan from the bank, a lease on a space, some purchased equipment, and a receptionist ... how hard can that be? That is how many clinical practices began and why many ended. In fact, the history of private clinical practice in Canada began with intrepid entrepreneurs hanging up their shingle on "Main Street" and hoping for the best. With some very hard work, great tenacity, and a corner on the market, many practices did make a go of it, and survived and prospered. Today, however, you may not want to hang your hat on that particular trial and error methodology.

The current health care environment is one of great upheaval and uncertainty. There is also an exponential increase in small private practices, and increasing competition from traditional and non-traditional practitioners. Given this context, a logical, carefully considered, and well-researched business plan may mean the difference between the success or failure of your practice.

4.1 Is a Business Plan Necessary?

You have two critical goals to meet to ensure that your business opens and both are met by devising your business plan. First, you must convince yourself that the business is viable and that it is what you want. Second, you must convince other interested parties that you know what you are doing and that your business concept has a good chance of being viable. Use the development of your business plan to set your goals and test their feasibility.

TAKE HOME MESSAGE

The success of your business begins with a well-researched business plan.

Corollary: The plan is a working document; revisit and revise it regularly.

A business plan is functional and dynamic. The plan provides both the basis on which you manage your business, and benchmarks and standards by which to measure progress and evaluate changes.

Not convinced? A business plan is your roadmap to your preferred destination. Without this map you are not likely to arrive at your destination. Developing the map helps the creator ensure they can interpret it and navigate by using it. Then with the map in hand, you not only get to where you are going but you can avoid running out of gas, as well as navigate around road hazards; if well conceived, it will get you there on time and in good condition.

Researching and completing a business plan:

▶ commits you to formulating clear goals and objectives;

▶ leads to knowledge (of the sector, your competitors, your customers);

▶ organizes the process, making a missed step less likely;

▶ tells you how much money you need for start-up and for ongoing operation;

▶ is required by the bank in order to provide you with financing;

▶ starts the process of linking you with professional advisors and consultants;

▶ highlights the risks, thereby allowing you to eliminate or minimize them;

▶ tempers entrepreneurial optimism with a measure of objective reality; and

▶ inspires confidence in yourself, lenders, and potential customers and referral sources.

See Appendix 1 for the business plan outline and enclosed CD-Rom for examples of business plans.

4.2 Breaking It Down – Just Fill In the Blanks

Here is where the fun begins. Take your ideas and put them down. Take your questions and answer them. Determine the risks and minimize them. Your plan is the place to point out the strengths and the weaknesses of the venture. Put everything on the table and then build on the strengths and mitigate the risks. Table 4.1 illustrates the skeleton of our recommended business plan.

4.3 Tips to a Successful Business Plan

▶ Be clear: use lay language whenever possible and avoid hyperbole.

▶ Be brief and concise: get to the point.

▶ Be honest and transparent: what you and the reader don't know will hurt you.

▶ Use lists, tables, charts, graphs, and illustrations to clarify.

▶ Explain any assumptions made.

▶ Substantiate any claims made.

▶ Be conservative in your estimates.

▶ Avoid redundancy: the only time we should see the same information twice is in the executive summary.

▶ Use appendices for the details (e.g., financial assumptions, floor plans, maps, demographic data).

▶ Package the plan professionally: editing, formatting, printing, and binding.

▶ Include a statement of confidentiality to protect the business' name, ideas, and research findings.

Table 4.1 The Business Plan Outline

▼ Business Plan Section	▼ Section Details
Title Page	Company name, address, telephone and fax numbers, Web and e-mail address, company owner(s), and key company contact names and titles.
Table of Contents	Major headings and minor subheadings referenced to page numbers.
Executive Summary	A concise one to two page summary of key points in the plan including financial projections.
Context	Background information to set the stage: what, why this, why you, why now?
Strategy	An overview of what the business will look like upon opening, for the three years of the business plan, and for five to ten years into the future; focuses on your Mission Statement and Vision Statement; introduces the concept of the "Go Criteria" (Hopkins-Rosseel, 2003).
Environment and Market	What is happening in business, health care, and your sector of health care?; What is on the horizon that may change the current environment and affect your business?
Industry and Customers	In your chosen geographic locale, what is your niche? What are your referral sources? Who are your potential customers (demographics and epidemiology)?
Services and Products	Details the proposed services, including who (client served), what services and products, and how the services will be provided.
Management and Staffing	Ownership and management details; names and contact information for how the business will operate (organizational chart, staff roles, and responsibilities); business' legal status.
The Location	Describes where you will be providing your services both geographically and in terms of the layout of any venues involved (equipment requirements also described).
Marketing Plan	Detailed account of pre- and post-opening promotions, and marketing strategy (includes an implementation plan and ongoing evaluation of the success of each strategy).
Financial Statements	Three year cash flow forecast; three year predicted income and balance statements (detailed financial assumptions upon which the predictions have been made).
Regulatory and Professional Issues	List key pieces of legislation and professional regulations affecting your proposed business; briefly describe current and predicted future professional issues affecting your business; note the possible impact of the legislation, regulations, and issues on your business.
Confidentiality and Recognition of Risks	Honestly detail foreseeable risks (financial, legal, professional, personal); outline all steps taken to mitigate those risks (purchases, policies, procedures).
Appendices	Detailed financial assumptions, demographic data, maps, lists, contact info., glossary, etc.

Hopkins-Rosseel, D. (2003). Developing a business plan: Scratching the surface. Presentations at the Canadian Physiotherapy Association National Conference. Toronto, ON.

CHAPTER 5
Focussing on the Process
DIANA H. HOPKINS-ROSSEEL,DEC, BSC(PT), MSC(REHAB), MCPA

5.1 *How* Do I Get Started?

Skim through Part I of this book from beginning to end to get an overview of the path being laid out for you. Then return to this chapter to work on creating your business plan. It is suggested that any successful health care private business will take a minimum of three to six months to plan and implement. While you read through these guidelines and descriptions, use the sample business plans on the CD-ROM provided to see how these pieces might look in a real context. Another tip: get your financial spreadsheets loaded and running (also on the enclosed CD-ROM as templates for your use), and put in costs whenever you make your tentative decisions. This will help to keep you grounded and make your business proposal feasible. (Refer to Chapter 14 "The Financial Plan: Starting and Ending Up Here," for more on spreadsheets.)

5.2 Dropping "a time-line"

A typical business plan covers six or more months of planning prior to opening your doors, plus projections for the first 3 years of operations. Here are some recommended steps to follow during the planning process.

1. **Create the skeleton of your business plan on your computer.** There are numerous Web sites that allow you to do your business plan in a stepwise fashion; experience has shown, however, that these rarely work for health care-based or service-based businesses. We recommend you start from scratch to allow you to be flexible and creative.

2. **Load the financial spreadsheets from the CD-ROM we have provided onto your computer.** If your business is primarily service based, use spreadsheet version 4.0. If your business is expected to have product sales as a measurable element, use the Cost of Goods (COG) spreadsheet version 2.0.

3. **Buy or create a blank 18-month calendar** with plenty of space to plan future tasks and record completed tasks.

4. **Start working through your business plan development** using Part I of this book as a guide.

5. **Keep track of your activities on the calendar using a different colour for each major category of activities** as you go through the business plan development. These include finance, human resources, marketing, location, and operations (keep some white-out handy for the inevitable changes!).

6. **Target an opening date and work backwards from there.** For instance, when you get to the chapter on marketing (Chapter 13) and you are devising a variety of approaches, each type will take a specified length of time to optimize the effect. A mailing with follow-up calls and visits to potential referral sources is a two-month process, and is generally completed one month prior to opening. So back up three months on your calendar and mark in projected start and completion dates. On the other hand, a media advertising campaign usually begins just before opening (when you are confident of your opening date), and runs three months to a year into operations.

7. **Start to formulate the concept of your future business** beginning with: (1) key background information on you and your ideas; and (2) the minimum criteria for plan implementation (the "Go Criteria©").

TAKE HOME MESSAGE

Take it one step at a time.

Corollary: There is no time like the present!

And now it begins ...

CHAPTER 6
The Context
DIANA H. HOPKINS-ROSSEEL,DEC, BSC(PT), MSC(REHAB), MCPA

A marketing expert comes into a room of senior occupational and physiotherapy students and asks each group a simple question: "What is occupational therapy?" and "What is physiotherapy?" After ten minutes it is clear that not one student is able to convey the essence, the scope, or the definition of their future profession succinctly and yet comprehensively. The expert concludes that it will be very difficult to serve the public well if they cannot articulate what it is they do. A banker faces prospective business loan partners – a speech language pathologist and an audiologist – and asks what they have in mind. Twenty minutes later he is concerned about any loan because, although he is able to understand what it is they are proposing, he is not sure why they wish to establish a business.

Before launching into any small business venture, you need to be able to clearly and honestly articulate not just what the venture will be, but why you are the best person (or persons) to undertake it, and, just as soundly, what makes the environment ripe for this particular business idea at this time. Once you are able to put your ideas on paper, you do the research and write a business plan to convince yourself of its strength and feasibility, and you return to review the original venture definition and the background environment you thought would support it: you have then come full circle.

6.1 The "New Venture" Definition

"New venture" refers to a new business and not an existing one that you are buying. Compose a comprehensive yet concise description of the business type. By reading this short paragraph, the reader should have an initial picture of the business you are proposing (e.g., private-for-profit versus not-for-profit; sole proprietorship versus partnership; incorporated or not; community care versus a clinic site versus a consulting business; multidisciplinary versus limited scope of practice; etc.). No details are necessary at this time; they will come up in the sections to follow. Similarly, those primary unique aspects of the business that will have added value (or perceived added value) will be briefly touched upon here but developed at a later time.

Or

The "Business" Definition–Reinventing an Existing Business

There are many advantages to buying an existing business but before you do, you must avoid the perils of taking on a business you do not know inside and out. You must not only review the financials and operations of the business but you should also write a new and detailed business plan. In doing so, some of the hidden flaws will come to the surface. It also provides you with the opportunity to integrate your new ideas and personality into the fabric of the business. In addition, it will function as a guide for your initial years at the reins. Just as with a new venture, you will start with composing a description of the business.

TAKE HOME MESSAGE

First impressions are often lasting impressions.

Corollary:
The best idea is only as good as your understanding of it and its expression.

6.2 The Background: *Why?*

Here is your one chance to introduce yourself and your partners (why you?). Your business plan lets the reader know you have the characteristics of an entrepreneur, and what education or experience you have in both your clinical field and in small business. Follow with a rationale for this venture (why this?); Is it an under-serviced area? Is the client demographic changing? Are you proposing new methods? Continue the rationale with your perception of the timing (why now?). These are just brief indications of what will be justified with data in subsequent sections. Then bring this section to its conclusion with *an impact statement*: your perceptions of the impact of opening your business on the clients, the community, and/or the profession(s) involved (fact or faith?).

CHAPTER 7
The Strategy

In this section you outline for yourself and the reader, an overview of what the business will look like upon opening, for the three years of the business plan, and for five to ten years into the future. These sections are relatively short and to the point. You will spend much of the remainder of the plan detailing the data that support these early ideas and assertions. Remember that the strategy of how to implement, run, and develop a business is all tied in with entrepreneurship and you as the entrepreneur. For that reason, the reader should see your unique stamp throughout the building of your strategy.

7.1 The Mission Statement

This is one of the most vital components of the business plan and of the management of your business. The mission statement should be a clear and simple representation of the enterprise's core purpose – why it exists in the here and now. It communicates the organization's fundamental nature, values, and work. Your mission statement will be found in the practice's Policies and Procedures Manual for your employees to read and internalize. It will be framed on the walls of the office or clinic for your customers to see, and incorporated in some way into your business stationery and marketing tools. It is a statement written in the present tense (as if the business was up and running) and exemplifies your goals for the practice. Avoid any professional jargon or current trendy terms or phrases in your mission statement.

Many businesses have a single, one-line mission statement, accompanied by a list of values as a separate entity – either approach works. As a single statement, or as two linked pieces, a clinical practice mission statement should contain a majority of the following elements:

▶ client population (e.g., "… of all ages …," "… high school, community-college, and university athletes …," "seniors, individuals with workplace injuries, …");

▶ focus (e.g., orthopaedics or pain relief);

▶ spectrum of care (e.g., "… from rheumatology to injury through post-operative care");

▶ commitment to quality (e.g., "excellence," "exemplary," "highest quality," "optimal," …);

▶ effectiveness (e.g., the use of outcome measures, evidence-based practice, best practices, …);

▶ efficiency (e.g., same-day service, 48-hour referral turnaround, triage process, …);

▶ philosophy (e.g., "client-centred") and the ethical position of the business (e.g., "honesty and integrity," "social responsibility," "transparency," "confidentiality").

If a mission statement works, it should answer your future practice questions. For instance, when the question comes up regarding whether or not to expand the size of the clinic, or open a second one, if the impact of doing so continues to allow you to fulfill your mission, then it is a viable option. If not, either you don't make the change or you revisit the mission of your business. More fundamentally, on a day-to-day basis, this compass may help you to choose between two prospective employees, decide how to triage your clients, or even choose what wall colours will reflect the ambiance you aspire to.

Try handing your Mission Statement to a layperson, and see if they understand and would feel inclined to become a customer. If the answer is "no" to either question, take another stab at the statement.

7.1.1 Example Mission Statements

Mission statements vary widely in their scope and length. Take, for example, this one from Merck Pharmaceuticals:

" ... to preserve and improve human life.

- ▶ Corporate social responsibility
- ▶ Unequivocal excellence in all aspects of the company
- ▶ Science-based innovation
- ▶ Honesty and integrity
- ▶ Profit, but profit from work that benefits humanity."

It is a terrific idea to get on the Internet and search for mission statements and vision statements. You will come up with a wide variety from a multitude of sectors. Pair those down to those in the small business sector and, finally, the small business health care niche.

You want to be comprehensive but not detailed or too lengthy. You are looking for both content and tone. This next one is from the rehabilitation sector. Notice how it is laudable for being thorough but is verging on being too wordy.

TAKE HOME MESSAGE

Every business has a reason for being.

Corollary:
To communicate is to share; to listen is to understand; to value is to commit.

A Rehabilitation Private Practice:

" ... to provide outstanding orthopaedic and neurological physiotherapy services to families in the greater Killington area. We are committed to evaluations and treatments based on the best scientific evidence provided in full collaboration with our clients. Our staff values our client's time and personal therapeutic goals. We provide confidential services with care and the ultimate goals of the client's optimal function and independence."

In the end, rehabilitation mission statements must be more than less because we are less well known and understood than many other markets. It is a chance to advocate as well as inform.

7.2 The Vision Statement

Whereas the mission statement is the present, the vision statement focuses on the future. This statement is more far reaching, outlining what you want your business to be. It is your inspiration and the framework for all your strategic planning. Unlike the mission statement, which is for the client's benefit, the vision statement is for you and the members of your business. It allows you to forecast what changes you envision making as the business grows or renews itself. The vision will have a significant impact on decision making and the allocation of resources; consequently, the vision statement of a small dynamic business generally extends at least three to five years into the future. Services (and products) that you anticipate changing or maintaining over time are presented here. For example, you may wish to start small, as a sole clinical practitioner, but you have every intention of growing with the demand. In this case you would state that fact, and indicate that growth will include additional staff, or more practitioners in your field, or adding practitioners from other fields. It would include indicating if operations are to change, such as increasing the size of the clinic or starting a satellite service. Similarly, if you plan to take on any "associates" who will share in the management and profits, this should be indicated. The details of when, how, and on what criteria these decisions are based, come after the comprehensive description of services provided and within subsequent sections of the business plan.

For a vision statement to be active and work for the business, each stage of development must be linked to benchmarks – markers for change. In the case of expansion for example, you may wish to use the length of time clients are on your waiting list as a marker to add staff. A financial marker may be one where the addition of more square footage or services may only be pursued when a designated annual net profit has been realized for a stipulated number of years. Similarly, taking on new services might be triggered by a needs survey or an ongoing influx of requests for that service. If you plan to increase clinical staffing, indicate what you would base the addition(s) on. For instance, when the waiting list meets or exceeds three weeks, three times in a quarter or for three or more continuous weeks, then you would hire one 0.40 full-time equivalent (FTE) physiotherapist and one 0.5 FTE physiotherapy assistant. Or perhaps you hope to diversify your services. You could stipulate that once you have passed the financial "breakeven" point, and have subsequently seen steady profits for at least six months, you will bring on associates in vocational rehabilitation. If you are a sole practitioner who provides services in the community, you may foresee a time when you open clinic space to service your more mobile clients or better meet the needs of your referral sources. If so, you could indicate that you will implement a needs survey process at the outset, gathering information on requests made for your services; specific demand level would be the impetus for you to open a clinic site.

Equally important are the outcomes. The methods of measuring the outcomes of the new growth are also built into the process and the vision statement. For example, the monitoring of the caseload of a new employee, or use of a new space are common methods of service evaluation. And, of course, the regular review of the cost of the new service versus the income from the service is a key element in determining the success of a business change or expansion.

7.2.1 Example Vision Statements

Bill Gates for Microsoft:

"There will be a personal computer on every desk running Microsoft software."

A Rehabilitation Private Practice:

"... to be considered the occupational therapy service provider of choice by regional referral sources as measured by bi-annual surveys to family physicians and local health care institutions. ... to attain a net profit of 15% of costs within three years of start-up. All profits up to the 15% will be held in a contingency fund, while those exceeding 15% of costs will be reinvested in the business through maintaining employee satisfaction, achieving optimal evidence-based practices, and expanding services. These resources will be allocated in priority order as follows:

1. 2.5% to each partner as profit-sharing as per the partnership agreement;

2. salary increases of inflation plus 1.25% to all employees past their probationary period;

3. staff development fund increases – allocation based on years of experience plus years with the company;

4. addition of prosthetic services and relevant resources (equipment and space).

7.3 Key Features

This section gives you the opportunity to highlight which elements of your expertise, education, experience, human resources, equipment, services, or site make your business unique in your environment, valuable to your customers, and attractive to your investors. This could range from your hours of service (e.g., extended and weekend hours) to a particular service provision (e.g., acupuncture or physical demand analyses and functional capacity evaluations).

A critical last piece of the strategy …

7.4 The "Go Criteria©"

When you buy a house you go house-hunting with a clear idea of what the structure and property must have before you will even consider putting in an offer. Do you have to have a garage or can you live without it? What about a fireplace? How many bedrooms will make the deal? Starting a business is no different. You need to make a decision about what your absolute minimum criteria are for going forward with the venture. These are called the "Go Criteria©".

For example, you will only go ahead once the following minimum but vital criteria are met:

▶ securing a term loan of $50,000

▶ securing a line of credit (operating loan) of $75,000

▶ each partner committing to a personal investment of $25,000

▶ finding a clinic site that is fully accessible

▶ a site that has free and ample parking

▶ a site that is at street level with walk-by traffic

▶ a landlord commitment to a lease with a non-competition clause

▶ a site on public transit

▶ committed referral sources from five physicians

The Go Criteria© list will differ with each individual business endeavour.

7.4.1 Example of Go Criteria©: Kevin and Asha

Kevin and Asha decided to start a speech language pathology and audiology clinic in town. They were long-standing colleagues and both knew intuitively that the need existed in the community. They put together a basic plan and dove right in. They found a location, pooled their savings to be used for rent and equipment purchases, consulted a lawyer, hired a receptionist, and opened their doors for business. Unfortunately, they had to endure a labour strike, which delayed the opening by three weeks. In the first month, they received 11 referrals, which increased to 23 in the second month, and 35 in the third month. By the third month, however, they could not pay their receptionist. They had projected 40 referrals per month as breakeven but had not factored in the slow start-up usually experienced by new businesses. Fortunately, Asha's father provided them with a temporary loan to tide them over.

What Kevin and Asha should have done before opening, was to put in place contingency plans with the related Go Criteria©. In this case, a line of credit to draw on in a funding crunch would have been prudent.

TAKE HOME MESSAGE

Hope for the best but plan for the worst.

Corollary: Everything is negotiable!

Once Kevin and Asha began the practice they found that, although they had soundproofing installed in the necessary spaces of the clinic, there were periods when adjoining rental spaces had construction or other activities going on that disrupted effective assessments and treatments of their clients. In this instance, a Go Criteria© of negotiating an isolated rental space or a cease and desist on construction work in adjacent spaces may have been possible.

CHAPTER 8
The Environment and the Market (Macro Analysis)

DIANA H. HOPKINS-ROSSEEL,DEC, BSC(PT), MSC(REHAB), MCPA

Here is where you jump back to the perspective you
gained in Chapter 2 regarding the Canadian health
care environments and position your particular business
within that context.

Heather planned to be an occupational therapy consultant working out of a home office. While putting together her business plan, she discovered that the Ministry of Health was reviewing community service funding models. With a little more investigating she learned that one of the initiatives was to increase funding allocation to assistive devices programs, in particular, computer-based systems to help individuals with a disability stay in their own homes. Armed with this knowledge she was able to write her plan to reflect that she would provide those services. She subsequently found those referral sources and, using her business plan, was able to get them committed before starting her business.

If you set up a business without knowing the national, provincial/territorial, and municipal economic, political, and social environments around you, there is a much greater chance you will not position yourself strategically enough to survive. This does not consist of merely collecting information; it is essential that you analyze the potential impact of your findings on your proposed business and that of the businesses around you.

8.1 Environment: Health Care Environment

Start with the overall health care environment. What are the trends in public versus private health care funding? Are there any current and proposed legislation, commissioned reports, or upcoming elections that may have an impact on your proposed business? If you wish to have a practice in canine therapy, does the absence of the legislated right to primary referral and the mandate to work through a veterinarian's referral bode well for the practice? Is a government's emphasis on primary care initiatives or the public funding of long-term and community care a benefit or a barrier to your potential earnings?

8.2 Market Analysis

The regulation and funding of health care is primarily provincial/territorial in Canada. Therefore, the focus should be on the provincial/territorial private sector analysis. Start with provincial/territorial trends and finish with a look at your own region: that is, delineate your niche in the market. Then undertake the necessary market research to determine the size of the industry, key market segments, key industry trends, and the industry outlook. More simply put: How many private rehabilitation practices are there in the province/territory? Has this number increased, decreased, or been stable over the past decade? What are the numbers for your niche (e.g., there may have been an exponential increase in private sector orthopaedic physiotherapy clinics and occupational therapy private consultants in workplace and insurance sectors, but cardiac rehabilitation multidisciplinary services began receiving public funding with the new government)?

Official government policies and documents can be researched on the Web. Government sources include the Ministries of Health, the Canadian Institute for Health Information, and Statistics Canada. Your regulatory body will also often publish their trends, data, and observations, as will your national and provincial /territorial professional associations. Look for experts in the field you are proposing to enter and those in health care policy. Read the newspapers or news sources on the Web daily to keep up with developments.

TAKE HOME MESSAGE

The key is in the "analysis" of the information.

Corollary:
Don't believe everything you read or hear.

CHAPTER 9
The Industry and Customers (Micro Analysis)

DIANA H. HOPKINS-ROSSEEL,DEC, BSC(PT), MSC(REHAB), MCPA

This is where we get into the nitty gritty of your business in the geographic location you have chosen. Determine how far your customers can and will travel, as well as where your best referral sources may be, and then do your micro analysis of that small corner of the world.

9.1 Competitor Analysis (Within and Outside the Profession)

9.1.1 Who Are Your Competitors?

Think both narrowly and broadly. Narrowly, your competitors are those who are currently doing what you plan to do. If you are a speech language pathologist partnering with an audiologist to provide a full range of diagnostic services, who else provides those services within a three-hour travel radius of your proposed clinic site? If you plan to provide regular intervention services, the radius may be reduced to a 45-minute one. Perhaps you plan to provide mental health services; then your competitors will range from regulated social workers, family physicians, nurse practitioners, psychologists, and psychiatrists, to unregulated counsellors and life-skill coaches. In the area of pain relief, the competitors are found in an equally broad spectrum, from regulated physiotherapy practitioners to unregulated hypnotists and Chinese medical practitioners.

9.1.2 Where Are Your Competitors? What Services Do They Offer? What Are their Standard Fees? Do they Have a Waiting List? If So, How Long is it on Average?

Create a list of your competitors in table format providing their name, location, services offered, and fee schedule. It is also helpful to know how long they have been in business; the longer they have been in business, the greater their hold on the market. In an appendix, produce a map with all competitor locations indicated (try direct competitors in one colour and other competitors in another). Remember, tables, lists, and illustrations are often the most easily digested information sources. Once you have the list/table and the map, analyze it with respect to your proposed location(s) in that city or region and your proposed services. Is your proposition feasible? Do you need to make modifications?

9.2 Customer Analysis (Referral Base, Revenue Sources, Clientele)

9.2.1 Who Are your Customers?

They will usually come in three categories: (1) your clientele/patients; (2) your referral sources; and (3) all revenue sources. It seems clear-cut that your patients or primary clients are your customers, but you must not lose sight of the fact that your referral sources are also considered your customers. You may have physicians, dentists, nurses and nurse practitioners, rehabilitation professionals, and other health care practitioners as referral sources. In addition, insurance practitioners, workers' compensation bodies, and corporate institutions may also send you referrals. Added to the mix is the complication of who actually pays for the services you provide. For example, your client Mary may be self-referred and pay out-of-pocket for her treatments; on the other hand, Ngo may have been referred by his family physician after a motor vehicle collision where he will have mixed MVA and private insurance coverage for the fees. You will need to have a good handle on all of these groups.

For your patients and primary clients, research that population's demographics. A physiotherapist planning to practice sports therapy in a smaller city with a rapidly increasing geriatric population, may have a vastly different business outcome than if s/he located the business in a large urban centre with national sports teams, a university, colleges, and multiple high schools. Your research will draw out age, injury and illness, and socio-economic demographics. If the population's members are largely unemployed, do not have extended health insurance, and set other priorities for their disposal income, it will be significantly harder to keep a business financially sound. Use Statistics Canada, government reports, and municipal Web sites to tease out the data.

Once again, we recommend creating lists and/or tables to document and illustrate potential referral sources, and the primary third-party payer groups you are likely to access. As you search out these resources, be sure to keep a record of their company name, key contact names, addresses, telephone and fax numbers, e-mail addresses and Web sites. The company name list can go in your business plan with a reference to the appendix holding the remainder of the contact information.

TAKE HOME MESSAGE

Simple, directed demographic research will set the stage for success.

Corollary: Don't open the box until you are ready to jump in.

Chenoa Wuttunee studied to become a physiotherapist in Ontario but wanted to return to her home province of Saskatchewan and provide primary and secondary prevention services to First Nation People in a rural region of the province. When she first looked at the data it was clear that, although her chosen demographic of individuals with diabetes, obesity, and cardiovascular disease was significant in size due to high levels of un- and under-employment, this population could not finance even a small not-for-profit multidisciplinary clinic. Her next step was to search for additional funding sources. What she discovered were significant national and provincial/territorial small business start-up grants, and numerous unanswered calls for proposals to support ongoing operational funding for native health services. With a few more phone calls to local physicians and remote specialists, she made the final discovery that those specialists in remote urban centres would not only commit to referring their patients, but would also commit to providing on-site medical clinics monthly!

CHAPTER 10
Your Services: *What* Will You Offer Your Clients?
DIANA H. HOPKINS-ROSSEEL,DEC, BSC(PT), MSC(REHAB), MCPA

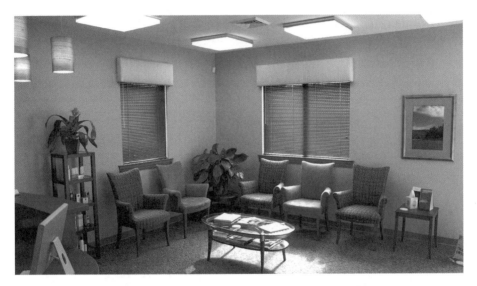

Now is the time to give a detailed description of all your

proposed services (and products).

The first step is to demonstrate the depth and breadth of your target populations: Who do you anticipate will benefit from your personnel, their skills and expertise, and your methods? Individuals with neuromuscular disabilities? Mental health clients? Individuals with orthopaedic and/or sports injuries? What is the age range? Paediatrics? Adolescents? Adults and/or seniors? What parts of the continuum from acute to sub-acute, rehabilitation, chronic care, and long-term care are appropriate? Primary care? Primary prevention? Secondary prevention and/or maintenance or palliation? Will you be located in a clinic or out in the community?

What range of services do you plan to offer? If your business is clinical, you may indicate that you provide assessments, prescriptions, education, treatment interventions, and return-to-work plans. If the business is more consultative, you may describe your services as evaluations, reports, consultations, and recommendations.

The next level of detail relates to goals and is often predominantly client-centred. For instance, you may wish to highlight that you provide pain relief, and/or early return to work, decreased employee sick days, palliative care, or independent living at home.

The deepest level, and the most difficult to navigate early in your planning, is the "How." What do you do that will accomplish your stated goals and those of your clients? This piece may be delineated in the larger elements in the body of the plan (e.g., relaxation therapy, modalities, soft tissue techniques, manual therapy, education), with the detailed breakdown in an appendix (e.g., progressive muscular relaxation, visualization, stretching, ice, heat, ultrasound, transcutaneous electrical nervous stimulation, interferential; individual and group education of the client, their family, and community supports). The easiest way to outline your services is to provide comprehensive lists and/or tables of each and then use a glossary of terms in an appendix to elaborate on the services that would not be familiar to the lay population.

As you try to complete this section you will have a chance to really understand, and limit or expand, the scope of your proposed products and services. Jot down some notes along the way regarding the space, equipment, human and financial resources that these services might require. This will not only accelerate completion of some of the upcoming sections but, more importantly, it will start to reveal the strengths and shortcomings of your plan.

> Some basic tenets of small business management suggest that to be too small and homogenous is to risk extinction, yet to be too diversified is to risk mediocrity in most things and excellence in few.

10.1 Try Something Like This on for Size ...

Table 10.1 Description of the Proposed Client Base for a Large Multidisciplinary Practice

▼ Potential Clients based on Proposed Service Provision	
Age Span	paediatrics (1–12); adolescents (13–17); adults (18–65); seniors (66+)
Systems	musculoskeletal, neuromuscular, cardiac, respiratory, urinary
Example Areas of Care	• progressive neuromuscular diseases (e.g., muscular dystrophy, multiple sclerosis) • congenital disorders/deficits (e.g., cerebral palsy) • primary prevention lifestyle management (e.g., atherosclerosis, obesity, diabetes, heart attack, stroke) • vocational (e.g., return to work, ergonomics, risk management) • musculoskeletal injuries (e.g., sports injuries) • musculoskeletal disorders (e.g., osteoarthritis, osteoporosis)
Service Delivery Locations	(1) community based: • schools • industry • home care • long-term care facilities (2) on-site clinic

Table 10.1 continued

▼ Potential Clients based on Proposed Service Provision	
Levels of Care	• rehabilitation/secondary prevention • maintenance • chronic care • long-term care
Service Delivery Types	• individual assessments • individual consultations • individual treatment sessions • individual exercise prescription • group education • group seminars • group exercise with monitoring • employer consultations • school consultations • discharge planning
Service Providers	• occupational therapist • physiotherapist • dietician

Range of Services	• documentation (e.g., reports, letters, evaluation summaries)
	• expert witness
	• clinical assessments
	  ⮡ physical demands analysis, functional abilities evaluation, ergonomic
	  ⮡ physiotherapy
	  ⮡ occupational therapy
	  ⮡ nutritional/dietary
	  ⮡ risk factor analysis
	• clinical treatments
	  ⮡ pain relief (acupuncture, TENS, ice, heat, intraferential)
	  ⮡ ultrasound
	  ⮡ manual therapy (joint mobilizations and manipulations)
	  ⮡ soft tissue techniques
	  ⮡ neuro-facilitation techniques
	  ⮡ mobility training and safety
	  ⮡ exercise: ROM, strength, aerobic capacity
	  ⮡ splint fabrication
	  ⮡ orthotic fabrication
	• assistive device assessment and prescription
	• seating clinics

Table 10.2 Description of the Proposed Client Base for a Small Partnership

▼ Potential Clients Based on Proposed Service Provision	
Age Span	children (8–17); adults (18+)
Systems	musculoskeletal
Example Areas of Care	• musculoskeletal injuries (e.g., sports injuries) • musculoskeletal disorders (e.g., osteoarthritis, osteoporosis, repetitive strain injuries) • immune system dysfunction (e.g., rheumatoid arthritis)
Service Delivery Locations	on-site clinic
Levels of Care	• acute through rehabilitation of post-operative conditions • acute post-injury rehabilitation • sub-acute and chronic relapses/set-backs
Service Delivery Types	• individual assessments • individual treatments • individual exercise prescription, monitoring, and progression • group seminars
Service Providers	• physiotherapist • massage therapist

Range of Services	• clinical assessments
	  ⊢ joint
	  ⊢ soft tissue
	  ⊢ functional
	  ⊢ mobility
	  ⊢ postural
	• clinical treatments
	  ⊢ pain relief (acupuncture, TENS, ice, heat, intraferential)
	  ⊢ ultrasound
	  ⊢ manual therapy
	  ⊢ soft tissue techniques
	  ⊢ mobility training and safety
	  ⊢ exercise: ROM, strength, aerobic capacity
	• group educational seminars (on-site and in the community)
	• full range of documentation

The trick here is to be as clear as possible. If you are going to be running around sports fields here and abroad, your descriptions and lists will be drastically different than if you are performing audiology assessments in a single clinic, or if you are an occupational therapist sharing your time between home care provision and two long-term care facilities.

If you plan to have direct links to the community, then that should also be apparent in this outline. For instance, you may share a receptionist and some facilities with a local fitness centre, or you may work with government and not-for-profit agencies. For these links, add a line to your table for "Collaborations."

TAKE HOME MESSAGE

Diversification can bring strength and limit risk.

Corollary:
You cannot be all things to all people.

Dara, a physiotherapist, and Zale, an occupational therapist, work with individuals with neuromotor limitations. One of their most successful methods of treatment has been hydrotherapy. To make this a feasible treatment option, they have located their clinic within a government facility equipped with an indoor pool. Their landlord-tenant relationship with the facility, includes protected hours for their staff and clients to have exclusive access to the pool and its facilities. This geographic and functional link is pivotal and should be transparent to potential investors and clients.

A final note: for our purposes in this book, products are things you sell to people, which could include goods and services. In your business you may wish to provide goods as well as services to your customers. For example, a therapist working with individuals with upper extremity injuries may be selling splints to their customers. Although we address the sale of goods briefly in many of the subsequent chapters of the book, and with the "Cost of Goods and Services" (COGS) spreadsheets, this aspect of the business will not be pursued in depth to avoid diluting our primary goal of the business of health care service provision.

CHAPTER 11
Management and Staffing: *Who* is on Deck?

DIANA H. HOPKINS-ROSSEEL,DEC, BSC(PT), MSC(REHAB), MCPA

It is important for you and your potential investors to see that you have considered your human resource needs, and have thoroughly considered the management and administration of your business. It is even more important that you and your partner(s) fully understand and agree to the proposed operations of the business. The three primary reasons for methodically investigating this area are:

1. each partner, manager, and administrator must have a well-defined role to optimize efficiency and itemize responsibilities, thus avoiding duplication and/or conflict due to critical errors or omissions;

2. the human resource aspects of business are considered the most expensive component of the operational costs of doing business; operational costs will be over 80% of your total annual business costs;

3. you and your staff are the business; excellence here will lead to the "good will" that keeps a business viable and profitable. If salaries and benefits escalate, the financial consequences can be devastating to the business.

11.1 Ownership

List the name of the owner(s), credentials, job title(s), and contact information.

11.2 Human Resources

Human Resources (HR) is a field of expertise in itself. For smaller practices, you may navigate this area well on your own with some "free" advice from your municipality's business association, provincial/territorial government small business advisors, and other groups such as the Business Development Bank of Canada. If you start to get lost, there are small business advisors and HR consultants you can access and pay for more in-depth information (see Section 11.3).

The basics in HR management include legislation, staffing, and performance management. Let's take each one of these areas at a time ...

11.2.1 Legislation

The pieces of legislation related to small business alone may number over 60, depending on your jurisdiction! Therefore, you will need to access some expert advisors along the way to ensure your business and HR activities are legal. *Relevant legislation will include:*

1. Common Law (CL): This refers to "case law" where the law derives its authority solely from usages and customs of immemorial antiquity, or from the judgment and decrees of courts. CL may govern employment contracts, specify obligations of the employer related to pay for services or providing a safe workplace, or specify obligations of employees related to duty to obey, to use appropriate skills, to take care, and to act in good faith. Similarly, the important concepts of giving reasonable notice by employer and that of "wrongful dismissal" may also be set by precedent in your jurisdiction regardless of the specific piece of legislation that would otherwise have dictated that area of HR or employment practice.

2. Canadian and Provincial/Territorial Human Rights Codes: These relate to the equal protection of all individuals including those who work for and with you. To avoid contravening the Code without intending to, you must have policies in place to prevent and deal with harassment, accessibility, disability and accommodation, and equity in the workplace. The Human Rights Commission can help you here.

3. Employee/Employment Standards Legislation: Provincial employee standards acts apply to all employees but not independent contractors. The legislation sets the minimum standards for employee protection including minimum wage, vacation time, overtime, leaves of absence, and sick pay. Of note is that collective agreements often set higher standards and these may be the ones your prospective employees may be comparing your offer to. Look here for concrete details such as maximum work hours allowed per day and per week, or minimum pay for paid holidays.

4. Occupational Health and Safety Legislation: This type of legislation dictates that you must consider safety in the workplace, and put in place policies and procedures to protect your employees and your clients. These standards will cover equipment usage

and maintenance, first aid and medical emergency procedures, safety of your assessment and treatment tools (e.g., acupuncture needle storage and disposal), and employee infection control practices amongst many other requirements.

5. Pay Equity Legislation: This type of legislation often comes into play to a greater extent in larger businesses; however, it is important to know the stance of the government on "equal pay for work of equal value" and how to put it into play in your practice.

6. Workplace Safety and Insurance/Workers' Compensation Legislation: This legislation is provincial/territorial but essentially oversees workplace safety education and training systems, provides disability benefits, monitors the quality of health care, and assists in early and safe return to work.

7. Labour Relations Legislation: Labour relation acts generally govern labour activities in a unionized setting. Although it is rare that employees of a small private health care practice would be unionized, you may be functioning with those environments just next door so you may wish, at a minimum, to understand enough to help with recruitment and retention of employees and, at most, to protect your employees.

8. Income Tax Legislation: These acts help the employer recognize tax status of employee types, can provide tax relief to small businesses, and can result in significant sanctions or fines if an employer contravenes the tax laws.

You need to know your legal rights and responsibilities, and those of your employees in all of these areas before you open your doors.

11.2.2 Staffing
Lets look at a few key questions that will get you to rough out your staffing needs ...

11.2.2.1 What Skills do you Need in your Professional Staff?
The answer begins with your Mission Statement and your overall business strategy. These are already mapped out so you need to start to define whom the practitioner(s) will be. Remember to consider staff mix and overlaps in scopes of practice.

11.2.2.2 How Many People do you Need?
To answer this question you need to know your business hours/hours of operation, space limitations, the complexity of the staff interactions, and the plans for coverage of meal times, breaks, education/professional time, vacations, and illness. To put a number to paper you might consider a few common practices in Canada. For example, most businesses describe staff complements in terms of full-time equivalents (FTEs) where 1.0 FTE = 37.5–40.0 hours/week of paid time. Although a 1.0 FTE employee who works an 8-hour day with an unpaid lunch period of 0.5 hours (e.g., 7.5 hours paid time), 5 days/week appears to offer you 1950 hours of work, this is actually 1837.5 hours after vacation time of 3 weeks. Subtract another 11 or 12 days for sick days or family leave and you are down to 1755 hours a year. When determining staffing levels, you also need to estimate productivity and what income is generated by each potential staff member. Even if the hours work, the income may not be sufficient, and you will have to go back and rework the numbers and the mix.

11.2.2.3 What Else Comes into the Staffing Mix?

Consider the skill sets: Are you looking for generalists or specialists? Think about the pros and cons of new graduates, their enthusiasm and up-to-date knowledge base, versus more costly but experienced clinicians. Another aspect of the decision-making process is the consideration of full-time versus part-time versus casual employees. Full-time positions tend to come with employee loyalty, retention, and consistent practice, but they may also limit your flexibility in light of fluctuating service supply and demand, and they may not meet your client's preferences for peak service hours. Part-time employees provide you with scheduling flexibility; the employee benefits from a better fit with their lifestyle. On the other hand, part-time employees may actually have less flexibility due to other commitments and they may be difficult to retain when full-time positions become available elsewhere. Casual employees allow the employer to have a bank of individuals who are willing to work for short periods of time to cover regular employee absences for illness, vacations, development time, and/or locums or leaves of absence.

11.2.2.4 What Are the Basic Staffing Costs?

Generally, when determining the annual cost of employment you consider two factors:

1. Salary: Usually based on an hourly negotiated wage and assumes that there is some level of coverage for paid leaves (e.g., statutory holidays, sick leave, education time, etc.). A variation on the payment of clinicians, employers will often pay on a fee-for-service (FFS) basis where the employee is paid for each client they provide service to, rather than by the hour. This is done to decrease costs to the employer and to reflect employee productivity.

2. Benefits: These can be negotiated with an insurance provider, with the owners and staff making choices regarding which services to cover (e.g., do you want dental or vision coverage, or both?), or may be provided as a lump sum monthly payment based on a percentage of salary. In small businesses the percentage in lieu may be as low as 10% compared to as high as 22 to 24% in unionized settings. If you are located near the larger settings, you may have to provide a higher percentage in lieu of benefits to be competitive.

11.2.2.5 Examples of the Cost of a Professional Clinician

(1)	Salary	1950 paid hours x $29.50/hour		$ 57,525.00
	Benefits	18% of the salary in lieu of benefits	$ 10,354.50	
	Annual Total			**$ 67,879.50**
(2)	Salary	1950 paid hours x $29.50/hour		$ 57,525.00
	Benefits	Semi-private hospital family coverage	$ 160.00	
		Extended health care coverage	$1,980.00	
		Dental – family	$ 765.00	
		Disability insurance	$ 860.00	
		Group life insurance	$ 235.00	
		Pension plan	$2,225.00	
		Canada Pension Plan	$2,560.00	
		Employment Insurance	$1,785.00	
		Employee Health Tax	$1,200.00	
		Workers' Compensation	$ 510.00	
				$ 12,280.00
	Annual Total			**$ 69,805.00**

11.2.2.6 What are the Hidden Costs?

In addition to the basic salary and benefits paid to employees, the employer must remember the various costs directly associated with service staff. These are sometimes referred to as "Loaded Labour Rates" or "Overhead Costs." They include employee training time and resources, the cost of absences due to injury or illness, service costs such as equipment maintenance, and costs of the space they use in terms of cleaning, heat, and utilities. These are covered in more detail in the chapter on financial statements (see Chapter 14).

11.2.2.7 What are Some Ways to Vary the Provision of Services?

Many rehabilitation practices use a variety of human resources (non employees) to offer a wider scope of services to the customer, without adding additional overhead or increasing the "loaded labour rate." Examples include sub-contracting services, outsourcing, and sharing of administrative costs. In these cases, you do not provide the services directly but, instead, find high quality services that your clients may need as an adjunct to your services and make legal contracts with those clinicians or companies to provide the services you don't. For instance, your client may have an upper extremity injury that you are treating but you have an agreement with a clinician in the community who fabricates the splint you have prescribed for the client. This way the client gets the splint but it is not necessary for you to provide the equipment or space required to make splints. Similarly, you could be located next to another rehabilitation provider but agree to share the reception space and receptionist functions, thereby adding the convenience of having a receptionist for more hours in the day while at the same time spreading the cost of a receptionist between two owners. As your business changes over time, such arrangements will be altered to reflect your needs and your finances.

12.2.2.8 What are "Associates" and How do they Fit In?

The term "associate" is not a legal one, in and of itself. Individuals in business coined the term to describe a contractual relationship that many small service businesses negotiate to help cover the costs of doing business. An associate usually negotiates a space-sharing agreement with the clinic owner who needs help paying the bills or has space available that is intended for future expansion. In return for the use of the premises (capital investment, electricity, receptionist, and telephone), the associate pays a certain percentage of his/her earnings to the business owner. Alternatively, the associate may pay a monthly flat rate. This arrangement means that associates do not meet the stringent guidelines of being independent contractors. Therefore, the business owner must be very careful and consult with a small business lawyer to ensure whether or not the associate might be legally deemed an employee, and determine if the owner must pay CPP, EI, and perhaps EHT and WC fees to an associate.

In a variation of the use of the term, an associate has come to mean a working investor in the business. In this case, the associate invests some money in the business and works as a clinician in the business. In this arrangement there is an expectation of some type of gain or advantage. In some cases this is the right of first refusal when the business is sold while in others, it is a small percentage of the net profits of the business. Again, these are murky waters and must be vetted by your lawyer and documented in a legal contract.

11.2.3 Employee versus Independent Contractor

An independent contractor (IC) is considered to be a self-employed individual rather than an employee. The Canada Revenue Agency (CRA) looks at this distinction from a tax standpoint and has laid out some guidelines to ensure that individuals who claim to be ICs are, in fact, classified as such, and are therefore eligible for the tax benefits inherent to that status. To determine if an individual is an IC you may apply five tests:

1. Test of Control: Generally, a great degree of control over the person's activities is indicative of an employer/employee relationship. If the organization sets the individual's hours of work, where they work, and how they work, for instance, the individual would likely be considered an employee. On the other hand, if the individual is given a specific task to accomplish, and has autonomy with respect to how the task is accomplished, as well as their hours of work, the individual could be considered an IC.

2. Integration Test: If the person's business does not have a separate identity from the organization they are dealing with, this could be indicative of an employer/employee relationship. This would be the case if the individual does not have a separate office away from the organization, and uses the equipment and stationery of the organization. If, on the other hand, a clinician had purchased their own tools and/or pays a negotiated amount for the use of the clinic's equipment and facilities, then they may be considered self-employed. If the person works on a regular basis, has only one contract, or one major contract, and this is the majority of their income, then they would likely be considered an employee.

3. Economic Reality Test: This concept deals with financial risk. If a person is truly self-employed, there should be the opportunity for profit and the risk of loss. If the organization has the right to get someone else to perform the work, the individual has the risk of decreased revenue. A self-employed individual would be required to pay for their own expenses, whereas an employee would probably be reimbursed for expenses incurred. Also, if the individual cannot be put in financial risk by faulty work of their own, this would be indicative of an employer/employee relationship rather than an IC. The primary indicator of financial risk is to have the IC pay a flat-rate fee, rather than a percentage of billings, for working within their facility or for their business.

4. Specified Results Test: An IC relationship usually pertains to the carrying out of a particular undertaking within a specified period of time. If the contract between the organization and the individual does not address the time frame of the relationship or the contract is for an indefinite period of time, it will be difficult to argue that the individual is an IC.

5. Organization Test: Is the person offering services in the context of a coherent business enterprise rather than merely putting him/herself in the service of a particular payer?

The CRA emphasizes that, while all five tests are important, one factor within the Economic Reality Test (number three) – that of a FLAT RATE fee paid by the contractor to the clinic owner – is an absolute requirement. Use of a percentage formula will automatically result in contractor status being overturned, because it does not involve the possibility of financial risk, something that is fundamental to independent contractor status. The onus is on the employer to make this distinction and to ensure that all rules relating to payroll are adhered to. The existence of a contract does not, on its own, assure clinicians of an IC status. Indeed, in several of the audits performed by the CRA, the auditors did not even review the contract, focusing instead on the "on the ground" features of the relationship between the clinic and the contracted practitioner. If the person being hired is an employee, the employer must pay Canada Pension Plan (CPP) and Employment Insurance (EI) premiums and, in some jurisdictions, the Employer Health Tax (EHT) and Workers' Compensation (WC) premiums. If an employer does not pay these premiums under the assumption that the practitioner they hired was an independent contractor and is found to be in error regarding the status of an employee, they will be liable for all back premiums with interest, plus any relevant penalties! The moral of the story is to assume anyone you hire is an employee until you apply these five tests and they meet the requirements. Once they do, ensure you have a detailed written contract outlining how they meet them, and keep regular documentation on how they continue to meet them in their ongoing practice.

Table 11.1 Advantages/Disadvantages of Independent Contractors

▼ Advantages of an IC	▼ Disadvantages of an IC
• low overhead	• contracts are finite putting stress on employee retention
• decreased stress on clinic finances, especially beneficial during start-up and growth periods	• clinic owner is vulnerable to the financial status/success of the business they are contracting from
• hours pre-determined by contract, giving work and lifestyle predictability	• the clinic owner must monitor the ongoing status of the contractor
• a high level of independence may be built into the contract	• if the contractor does not continue to meet the terms of the contract the clinic owner is liable

11.2.4 How Do I Determine my Staffing Needs?

One more chance to create a table! It is not enough to list your projected staff complement, you must look at the criteria you need to provide services, make human resource decisions, and get the business up and running.

Table 11.2 Staffing Arrangements #1

Title	Role(s)	Education	Duties	FTEs	Hours
Physiotherapist	• owner • administration • management • client care	• M.Sc. (PT)	• human resources • billing and bookkeeping • development and monitoring of policies and procedures • marketing • purchasing, leasing, and maintenance of equipment and supplies • clinic rental • clinic space design • client assessment, treatment, and documentation • liaison with insurance providers • health care provider communications	1.4	Client Care: Mon.–Fri. 8:00 am–7:00 pm
Kinesiologist	• PT Assistant • client care	• B.Sc. (Kin)	• client delegated treatments • client monitoring • client care area	1.0	Mon.–Fri. 8:00 am–4:00 pm
Receptionist	• reception	• High school certificate	• answer phones • client scheduling	1.0	Mon.–Fri. 8:00 am–4:00 pm

Do you see any flaws in this recommended staffing arrangement?

▶ The physiotherapist has 11-hour days for client care; therefore s/he will be undertaking the administration and management of the clinic by taking time away from client care or, more likely, in the evenings and weekends. This is a sure recipe for burnout.

▶ Perhaps there should be contract consultants for the bookkeeping, or other administrative or management duties that are well defined in both scope and timing?

▶ The receptionist is underutilized; this staff member could be hired with a college diploma in business, and undertake the billing and many of the administrative tasks. For a small clinic, the receptionist also often backs up the physiotherapy assistant as an aide for tasks that can be delegated.

▶ Staggering staff hours will serve clients better; the receptionist can have the clinic open and clients ready to be seen before the physiotherapist and kinesiologist begin client care. There should be overlap in schedules for team meetings and in-services, but the two hired staff could cover all of the PT's hours to ensure the PT is not alone with clients in the clinic at any time – this is important from an efficiency and liability point of view.

> If a staff member is qualified to perform some of the same tasks within a shared scope, then there is less disruption of the clinic services if a staff member is not available for any reason. Therefore, duplication of duties should likely appear in these lists.

Table 11.3 Staffing Arrangements #2

Title	Role(s)	Education	Duties	FTEs	Hours
Physiotherapist	• owner • admin. • management • client care	• M.Sc. (PT) or equivalent • courses in small business admin. and management	• human resources • bookkeeping • development of policies & procedures • marketing • equipment purchasing and leasing • clinic rental/leasing • clinic space design • client care • liaison with insurance providers • communications	1.0	Client Care: Mon.,Wed., Fri. 8:00 am –4:00 pm Tues., Thurs. 11:00 am– 7:00 pm Admin Time: Tues., Thurs. 7:30 am– 10:30 am Mon.,Wed., Fri. after 4:00 pm as required
Accountant	• consultant	• CGA • owns his/her own small business	• initial business accounting set up (format and software) • annual taxes • annual audit of the books		As required
Equipment Maintenance Consultant	• consultant	• CSA certified	• monthly, regularly scheduled equipment maintenance (only for purchased equip.) • on-call equipment repairs		As required
Kinesiologist	• PT assistant	• B.Sc. (Kin) Min. 2 years experience	• client delegated treatments • client monitoring • client care area • monitors policies and procedures including occupational health and safety items	1.0	Mon.,Wed., Fri. 8:30 am– 4:30 pm Tues., Thurs. 11:00 am– 7:00 pm
Receptionist	• client care • reception	• College Business Diploma min. 3 years experience	• answer phones • client scheduling • billing, accounts receivable • basic weekly bookkeeping • supplies and inventory management • liaison with insurance providers	1.0	Mon.–Fri. 7:30 am–3:30 pm

11.2.5 Performance Management

When managing your human resources you will have several key roles: (1) recruitment, selection, and hiring; (2) employee performance appraisal; (3) retention of good employees; and (4) remediation and possible subsequent firing of employees who do not meet the standards. It is strongly recommended that small business owners take periodic management courses to facilitate their roles as managers and thus foster an excellent work environment. Not only is employee management important to the functioning of the business, but it can also be very costly if done poorly. The cost to train a new employee is generally considered to be two to three times their annual salary to get the employee working at their maximum potential. Once you have brought a new employee onboard, you do not want to lose them!

Jennifer and her partner, Sam, agreed that Jennifer would handle the business' HR activities. Jennifer successfully hired an administrative assistant (AA) with bookkeeping skills and a rehabilitation assistant for the clinic. Within a month it was clear to both Jennifer and Sam that the AA was overwhelmed and was actually not as familiar with basic software applications as she had suggested. Jennifer decided to give her some leeway because they were all relatively new to private practice and, after some one-on one remediation, decided to leave things for a month or so. By the end of the second month, the AA was not showing any improvement and Sam was expressing increasing frustration with the situation. At this point Jennifer met with the AA again and tried to address both owners' concerns. The AA cried, promised to work on her weaknesses, and asked for another chance. Jennifer agreed. By the end of the third month in practice, it was clear that the AA did not have the basic skills to do her job, that there were complaints from referral sources, insurance providers and clients, and that Jennifer needed to act. Jennifer gave the AA her written notice of termination with two weeks notice. The next week the AA returned to work and Jennifer and Sam received notification from the AA's lawyer that she would be suing for "wrongful dismissal."

How could Jennifer and Sam's situation been handled better? At the outset, the two of them needed to work together and come to joint decisions on the framework for the clinic's HR. Here are some recommendations:

▶ Agree upon and document each employee's role and job description.

▶ Design the hiring process to allow you to fully assess each candidate's knowledge, skills, attitudes, and behaviours. This must involve reference checks, a behaviour based interview process and, whenever possible, both employers (and, when relevant, key staff members) on the interview panel.

▶ Ensure you have a probation period stipulated in the contract (usually three to six months but can be up to one year).

▶ Put in place a well-delineated performance review process of formal annual reviews plus frequent feedback sessions and remediation interventions during the probation period.

▶ Have formal performance appraisals based on known, agreed upon, measurable, valid outcome or behaviour indicators.

▶ Ensure that all performance concerns and interventions are communicated to the employee, acknowledged by the employee, and well-documented.

▶ Maximize staff communications with an open door policy to allow them the time and opportunity to communicate their needs and concerns, as well as any changes they have made to improve their knowledge or skills in an area of concern to you.

▶ Ensure performance appraisals include balanced feedback in terms of both positive actions and skills, and those that require improvement.

The best advice regarding personnel management is to think about how you want to treat your employees and colleagues and how you would like them to treat you. Then foster your approach by hiring individuals whom you believe will adopt and enhance that environment. Your vision can be translated into your Policies and Procedures Manual to help with the tough decisions. Remember, being honest, trustworthy, transparent, direct, supportive, flexible, and respectful does not translate into having lenient policies that lead to time-consuming, costly, and frustrating situations.

11.3 Do You Need Advisors?

There will come a time in developing and running your private practice when you will realize that your education didn't give you all the answers and that you need help! Consultants are advisors who offer specialized knowledge, skills, and expert advice not available within your business or from someone on your payroll. They help to prevent problems and help provide solutions to existing problems or those that may arise along the way.

In the end, business decisions predominantly come down to a cost-benefit analysis. On the benefit side, having input or assistance from a bookkeeper, accountant, lawyer, banker, insurance broker, architect/designer and inspector, an expert in marketing, and an information technology consultant will definitely maximize your potential for success. They will also help you to take on the multiple roles required of you as an owner. On the down side, this all costs money.

Let's take several in turn and note what rationale you might have for requiring their services.

11.3.1 Accountant

Accountants provide accounting and business advice to clients in areas such as small business tax, audit, information technology, personal financial planning, business valuation, receivership, insolvency, and forensic investigation. An accountant will help you set up your books, give you advice on government regulations, and do your annual audit and taxes. There are three major accounting designations: (1) Certified Accountant (CA); (2) Certified General Accountant (CGA); and (3) Certified Management Accountant (CMA). The CA program specializes in audits and taxes, and all have experience in public practice firms. The CGA program is more general and covers audit, financial accounting, tax, and management. CGAs have great technical skills, and are often found in public practice, working in CA firms or on their own. CMAs focus on managerial accounting and are most often found in industry. It is essential that you hire one of these professionally designated accountants because the term "accountant" may not be regulated in your jurisdiction.

11.3.2 Bookkeeper

In small businesses, bookkeeping clerks often handle all financial transactions and record keeping. They record all transactions, post debits and credits, produce financial statements, and prepare reports for the manager(s). Bookkeepers also prepare bank deposits by compiling data from payments, verifying and balancing receipts, and sending cash, checks, or other forms of payment to the bank. They may also handle payroll, make purchases, prepare invoices, and keep track of overdue accounts. A bookkeeper used on a regular basis, is no longer a consultant – he/she is an employee. It is usually much less expensive to pay a bookkeeper than an accountant so, if you do not wish to do your own bookkeeping, then hiring a separate bookkeeper, or an administrative assistant, or a receptionist with bookkeeping training and expertise, is a good investment. Regardless of who does the books, you are still responsible for checking them regularly and ensuring that the practices are ethical, legal, and are the best for your business.

11.3.3 Lawyer

A lawyer who deals with small business practices will be able to provide expert advice on the structure of your practice and on all contracts. Their input will be invaluable in the purchasing or leasing of a site. This is expertise you will not want to forego.

11.3.4 Banker

You will use a bank for two main purposes: to secure any necessary loans and to perform the business' banking, including deposits, payments, and short-term savings activities. When choosing a bank or trust company you need to investigate all your options. If you are going to approach the bank for a loan, find a branch that specializes in lending because they will have greater lending authority and flexibility. Watch out for extra charges for any and all banking transactions; some banks charge a fee to accept and review a loan proposal.

11.3.5 Architect/Designer and

Inspector

Choosing to use an architect or designer is a personal choice and will often depend on your experience, expertise, and comfort in going forward on your own with your clinic space design. If you don't have any past experience and you do not have access to reputable advice

TAKE HOME MESSAGE
Up-front expert advice will help avoid a crisis in the future.

Corollary: Often, the initial cost is nothing compared to fixing the problem later.

from a seasoned clinician owner, paying for this input may be worth it in the long run. If there is significant construction required, you will need a "stamp of approval" but in most jurisdictions, a registered interior designer may also provide this service. In addition, an inspector will usually perform a single site visit, which has the potential of protection you from serious physical disasters. Having the site report may also decrease your insurance costs.

11.3.6 Small Business and Human Resources Consultants
You will be able to find basic advice on small business planning and start-up in all areas from provincial/territorial and national government offices and Web sites, as well as from local municipal services such as the Downtown Business Association and members of the Chamber of Commerce. These are a very good start. What you may be missing are personal solutions and direction for your individual business. There is a wide variety of small business consultants and often, they are not regulated. If you need help, look for an advisor who knows health care, who has references from businesses that are similar to yours, and who is not duplicating the services your other advisors have to offer. If your lawyer is familiar with human resource legislation you may not need to go any further.

11.3.7 Insurance Broker
You will require one or more insurance policies covering life, disability, office protection, and liability. A broker will often help you to sort out what coverage you need and what company (or companies) provides you with the best coverage at the best prices. As an individual owner or partnership, insurance companies may not want to take a risk on your business due to high failure rates in the first three years of a small business. This is where being a member of a professional association is likely to get you good coverage at good rates. You may wish to use both a broker and access the company that works with your association, and compare the two options. Insurance can be tricky. Table 11.4 outlines the basic categories of insurance for small businesses.

11.3.8 Financial Planner
Financial planners may advise you on employer and employee benefits, investments, and/or insuring and protecting your assets. A Certified Financial Planner has met educational and experience requirements, successfully completed national examinations, adheres to a professional code of ethics, and participates in continuing education directed at ongoing competency. Read Part II of this book to see where this type of help may take you!!

11.3.9 Information Technology (IT) Consultant
We are into the era of e-commerce, electronic bookkeeping, client scheduling, and health care records. In addition, we have a strong mandate to ensure quality assurance activities and program evaluation. With such a heavy demand on our technology, you may wish to consult with an individual who can advise you on your hardware and software needs. Do you need wireless technology? Is wireless a risk for privacy protection? Should you consolidate your software by purchasing one-client management service or should you use your accountant's software for your financial and budgeting activities? Is an Internet-based software package a better option than installing a package on your hard drive? You

Table 11.4 Basic Categories of Insurance for Small Businesses

Insurance for Owners, Partners, and Key Employees

Life: This protects the family and is especially important in a sole proprietorship that is not incorporated because the owner is personally liable for all debts of the company.

Disability: This insurance is designed to cover income for up to 52 weeks. Because you are self-employed, you do not have a benefit package to cover life and health insurance. As someone whose livelihood depends on your health and ability to run your business, disability insurance is essential. Any payments made for disability, health, and dental insurance along with professional membership fees are tax deductible in most jurisdictions, further reducing the cost. Of course, then you do not claim the actual expenses because you will be reimbursed through your plan.

Critical Illness: This is a personal insurance policy that provides a tax-free, lump-sum benefit to a business owner if he/she is diagnosed with a critical illness (e.g., stroke, heart attack, or cancer).

Partnership: Designed to protect a surviving partner and the business by allowing him/her to purchase the shares of the deceased to continue the business and offset the tax liability that would otherwise exist without the buy-sell agreement.

Key Person: This policy covers the cost of the loss of an integral member of your business team if the essential person should be unable to work for a period of time.

Business Property and Liability Insurance

Vehicle: Your personal vehicle insurance will be inadequate if you use your vehicle for business purposes. It is essential to have a policy that includes the use of your vehicle for business to cover damage to your vehicle and any responsibility you may have to others.

Product or Service Liability: Protects you in the event you are sued by a client/customer for non-performance of a contract or a product, and any liability arising from the non-performance. As a clinician, you must carry professional liability insurance; this is generally available through your professional association.

General Liability: Covers injury to clients and employees on your premises or elsewhere, either in the performance of duties for the company or involving the activities of the company.

Business Premises and Contents: Whether your office is in your home or elsewhere, this insurance covers damage, loss, or theft of property. If you work from home, it is unlikely your basic house and contents insurance will be adequate. Be sure your existing homeowner's policy is not voided by the operation of a business on the premises.

may wish to canvass all the companies that have the software you are considering, listen to their pitches, then contact current users of their products, and current private practice owners for their input, and then make your own decisions. If this makes you uncomfortable, you may wish to find an IT expert familiar with private health care in your field and pay them for a couple of consultation sessions to review the options with you.

In most jurisdictions, lawyers, accountants, and many other professionals will provide you with the first half-hour to an hour of consultation free. This gives you a chance to compare your options and to see if they are a good fit with you, your partner(s), and your business.

11.4 Management and Administration

Now you want to demonstrate the levels and flow of responsibilities amongst the owners and staff. The most comprehensive way to depict this is by using an organizational chart. The brief role descriptions are already in the staffing table and the full role descriptions for each position on staff will be written out in full in the Policies and Procedures Manual. This allows us to use a simple chart as a way to summarize and clarify the relationships. Until the Policies and Procedures Manual is developed and approved, you will need to complete this section with a written section on the specific management and administration duties as well as responsibilities, ensuring smooth operations right from start-up and building confidence in potential investors.

In the example organizational chart below, the lines depict a reporting structure, not an employer/employee relationship. The hatched lines have been chosen to distinguish the relationship of a consultant or contracted service from the standard employee relationship. A key to allow the reader to understand the schematic with ease and at a quick glance accompanies these charts. In the case of professions where delegation of scope of practice is legislated, this chart may also be used with a colour key to add those relationships.

Figure 11.1 Example Organizational Chart

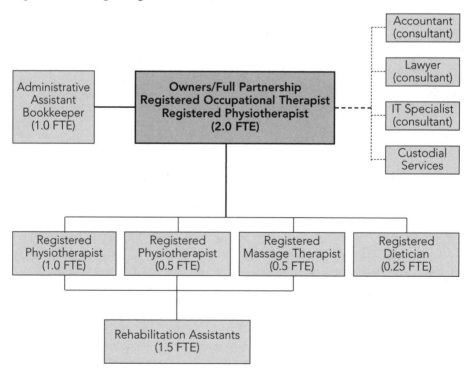

11.5 Labour Market Issues

Sven had a plan to start up a sole proprietor private practice with a part-time receptionist/bookkeeper and a casual rehabilitation assistant. His plan looked good and he received loans in the amounts applied for from the bank. Once the funding was secured, Sven began early marketing of the business to potential referral sources, and leased a small clinic space. Then the bottom fell out from under him. Six weeks before the scheduled opening date of the clinic, Sven was still without staff. He had not anticipated the fact that the region did not have college programs for office staff or rehabilitation assistants, or the fact that the unemployment rate was the lowest it had been in years. He soon realized that in order to recruit and retain staff for his clinic, he had to increase the salaries and benefits offered to applicants. This made for another trip to the bank and an increase in his operational loan to cover the unanticipated differences.

Sven's situation is actually not unique in small business. When deciding on what staff you would prefer to have in order to provide the services you would like to offer, a concurrent task is to look into where those individuals and professionals will be coming from. This includes not only how and where they are educated, and where they derive their experience from, but also the supply and demand trends for each category of staff member over the past few years. This approach is paramount to your overall recruitment and retention strategies.

This section provides the reader with all 3 necessary components of the labour marker issues in your niche and geographic location:

1. **What available pool you will recruit from (new graduates or experienced staff, local or distant sources);**

2. **What trends you can find in employment in your designated roles; and**

3. **How you intend to recruit and then retain those individuals.**

If Sven had planned his practice in a city/town equipped with a rehabilitation therapy school, a college with rehabilitation assistant and massage therapy programs, or an institute with small business course offerings, his dilemma would not likely have occurred. If there were a hospital in town that had recently had staff layoffs, again the problem may have been avoided. In the end, the approach is to research the staffing potential before moving any further with your plan and always finance your plan with a buffer for the unexpected.

TAKE HOME MESSAGE
Research staffing supply and demand trends before moving ahead with your plan.

Corollary: Look before you leap.

CHAPTER 12

The Location: *Where* Can They Find You?

DIANA H. HOPKINS-ROSSEEL,DEC, BSC(PT), MSC(REHAB), MCPA

12.1 Finding the Perfect Spot

Where should you locate your business? This can be a tricky question. If you are working on the road and out of your trunk, then the decision may hinge primarily on your convenience and cost. An office in your home is inexpensive, a tax write-off, and very handy. On the other hand, if you are planning a practice where your clients come to you, there will be many more variables to be considered.

What are the key considerations when choosing a private clinic setting? Here are some suggestions:

1. Accessible building and facilities
▶ regardless of what business you are in, if people are coming to your place they must be able to get in, get out, and get around the site without any physical barriers;
▶ other accessibility issues may include provisions for the hearing or visually impaired;
▶ included in this category is flexibility of "office hours" – don't get caught in a lease for a building that locks its main doors at 5:00 pm.

2. Public transit access
▶ depending on the population you are planning to serve, there is likely to be a greater or lesser need for transit access; it is unlikely that all of your clients have their own transportation;
▶ research has shown that a bus or subway stop more than a few steps away is a deterrent, so look for something very close.

3. Free parking

► the advantage of free parking alone is substantial to the success and competitive nature of a business; if your customers can't get to you quickly and easily, they will go elsewhere;

► this is a much more difficult situation in many urban centres; if you cannot find a reasonable rent and location where there is free parking, consider paying the parking for your clients with vouchers.

4. A marketing advantage

► having a "storefront" at street level where the driving and walking public pass by and see your establishment frequently is "free" advertising;

► the downside is that street level locations are usually more costly to rent and may have limited parking nearby.

5. Proximity to other health care practitioners or services

► department stores like to be located close to other department stores because they know that retail customers like to keep all their shopping within a small radius and are likely to try out both stores at that location;

► this holds true for the private health care sector; complementary services are a bonus to potential clients.

6. Your competition

► conversely, you do not often want direct competitors right next door unless there presently is, and will be in the foreseeable future, enough business demand for both of you;

► otherwise, direct comparison may make you look good today but put you out of the running the moment they add the next new thing before you do!;

► see if you are able to determine the weaknesses inherent in your competitors' services.

7. Your referral sources

► again, it is true that the clinic that is "out of sight" may also be "out of mind";

► it is not necessary to be geographically central to your referral sources (health care practitioners, industry, insurance provider groups), but it does provide you with many more unstructured opportunities to promote your services; this can be a huge advantage over time.

8. Your needs – size, facilities

► even if the location is right, the building or space may not be;

► you will need to have a good idea of the square footage you need and the layout of the space before you start looking for a location;

► if you plan to expand in the future, you will also look for sites where adjacent spaces may come up for lease, not those whose tenants have been there for decades!;

► if you have special needs, such as floor support for heavy exercise or testing equipment, soundproofing options for examination rooms, specialized electrical service, outside lawn space for therapy, or extra water supply for laundry facilities, you will have to factor in those aspects of your requirements as well.

9. Costs

► when it all comes down to it, despite great facilities in a great location, the site you wish to lease may be out of your price range – especially at start-up when outlay is huge and income is next to nil;

► playing "devil's advocate," on the other hand, you may want to spend more up front to promote a healthier business in the long run.

Here's where you retreat to your Go Criteria©. If you stipulated right at the outset that you had to have an accessible clinic, you will have to do what is necessary to search out that attribute in a location before you choose a final site. Weigh the pros and cons of every option before you settle on the best location for your services at that moment in time and for the near future. And don't hesitate to ask current and previous clinic owners what has worked for them and what errors they feel they may have made with their choices. You might be surprised with how honest and forthcoming many colleagues will be.

12.1.1 Everything's Negotiable!
Well, not really, BUT many things are. Look at all the decisions you are making and query the options for every single one of them.

Being fearless, and yet somewhat naïve about business, Steve went into negotiations to rent the third and best potential location for his private practice. It was slightly larger and more expensive than he felt he needed but the location was perfect. They were asking $8.50 per square foot or $27.89 per square meter (1 foot = 0.3048 meter) for the space. This looked like an exceptional deal compared to other prices he had been quoted. For the 1000 sq. ft. space he was considering, this would mean $13,600 a year, or $1,133.33 a month. He thought he had shrewdly negotiated the first two months rent free and signed on the dotted line for five years. Imagine how shocked he was when the monthly invoice for his rent came in at $2,321.66 a month!! And then there were the "leaseholds" ...

So, where did Steve go so very wrong? Before you negotiate and sign a lease for an office, a clinic, or any other practice space, you need to understand how leases are calculated and investigate the situation with the landlords at the properties you are considering.

12.2 What Kinds Of Leases are you Apt to Come Across?

A **Gross Lease** has the tenant paying a flat monthly amount, leaving the landlord responsible for all other common building operating expenses including heat and utilities, repairs, insurance, and taxes. This type of lease is becoming less common due to the rising cost of many of these expenses, especially those related to energy.

A **Net Lease** adds the cost of property taxes to the tenant's monthly rental fee. The tax fee may be a percentage of the overall real estate taxes depending on the landlord's arrangements for the tenants in the rest of the building. If the tenant must add insurance costs and taxes to the base rent, it is often referred to as a Net-Net Lease. Taking it one step further, Triple-Net Leases are applicable when all building operating costs are the responsibility of the tenant(s).

Percentage Leases are different again. If you are one of multiple tenants in a retail situation, such as a mall, you may pay a base rent plus a percentage of gross income.

The semantics are not important. What is important is that you know all the potential costs up front and determining who is responsible for paying them. For more information on business and signing a lease, check out the Canada–Ontario Business Service Centre at www.cbsc.org .

12.3 How Much is the Rent?

In Steve's case, he was paying $1,113.33 for a "net" space of 1600 sq. ft. plus an extra $255.00 for the "grossed up" space of 360 sq. ft. to cover the cost of a percentage of the common spaces in the building (e.g., hallways, public washrooms, lobby, and elevators). To this the landlord added an additional fee equivalent to $7.00 per sq. ft., or $933.33 a month, to cover a percentage of his costs for property taxes, building maintenance, cleaning of common areas, and building security measures.

TAKE HOME MESSAGE

Take the time to investigate all the options, permutations, and combinations for several potential locations before signing a lease.

Corollary: Those who dig come out on top!

Had Steve known what questions to ask and how that landlord calculates rents, he may have considered that having a fixed monthly rent of $2,321.66 was quite reasonable for a start-up business rather than not knowing month to month what some of those costs would be. On the other hand, he may have investigated what the cost of each of those items was, and he may have been able to procure them at lower rates himself.

As you think about the cost of renting a space, it is the opportune time to look into other service costs that protect you and your business. Although building landlords are often mandated by legislation in their jurisdiction to carry building **insurance**, they may carry only the minimum or only enough to protect themselves. You will usually carry your own insurance, not only including building insurance in case of flood, fire, or other disaster, but also coverage for equipment, liability, casualty, and any other risks you might anticipate at the outset of your business. For instance, can you cover the unexpected illness or absence of a key employee? You will need to have an expert advise you on what you need and how to make it fit with what your landlord and other tenants document they have. Insurance is costly, so carrying out a risk/benefit analysis is probably a good idea.

Who is cleaning the common areas, dealing with the recycling and garbage, shovelling the snow at the entrance, or maintaining the elevator? Is there a back-up electrical generator and/or emergency lighting? What security is in place for the building? These are good questions to ask. Sharing the decisions on these items might be something you wish to discuss. More importantly, you want to know how you, your staff, your chattels and records, and your clients are protected. Finally, who carries the burden of costs for these and how?

And there's more … Back to **"Everything's Negotiable."**

What are the options for the **term of the lease**? Leases generally run three to five years but may be negotiable up to 10 years. As a start-up business you may want the security of a five-year lease, thereby knowing what your costs will be. If so, make sure you try to negotiate an escape clause in the lease. If your business does not do well and you decide to close the doors, an escape clause will allow you to do so, with a certain amount of notice, with minimal financial loss. Taking a longer lease also gives you more room to negotiate because landlords like to have stable tenants. If the location of your business is key, push for a longer lease. On the other hand, a short lease gives you, the business owner, increased flexibility to pick up and move when you think the time is right. So, all other things being equal, you may opt for the shorter lease.

Rental increases may occur at the time of negotiation of the new lease or when a new tenant moves in. This may be best for you, although it is becoming less common. It is more likely that the landlord will insert an annual increase in the rent – an escalation clause – or charge you an estimated increase for operational costs, then calculate any extra fees or rebates to the tenants at year end.

Another area for negotiation is free rent or lower monthly rent for a couple of months. If the rental market is "soft" and landlords are short of customers, or if you are willing to sign a longer-term lease, the landlord will often consider sweetening the deal by giving you one to three months free rent. These types of landlord concessions are quite common.

This leads us to the **start date** for the lease and for the opening of your doors to the public. You will need to have a firm start date as well as a clause in your lease indicating that you are not responsible for any rent or other building costs if any delay in opening is due to the landlord's areas of responsibility. If he is contracting out any new construction or space improvements to be done prior to opening and they are not complete, this will cost you in lost fees for service, and in lost "good will" with your referral sources and customers. You may even be able to negotiate a **tenant allowance**, that is, a decrease in your rent or a deferral of your rent, if you are not able to take occupancy on the start date due to unforeseeable delays on your side of the operation. Examples might be that your equipment supplier is late with delivery, there is a labour strike at the source of your supplies, or a key staff member is late in relocating.

What do you do if the size of the space is right but you want to make changes to the internal layout of the space? These changes are often referred to as **"leasehold improvements"** and take the form of anything from re-wiring, to taking down or putting up new walls or room dividers, wall coverings, floor coverings, and/or bathroom or kitchen plumbing installations. This area of the lease may be the most open to negotiations. On the one hand, these changes are often costly and may not be seen as "improvements" by the landlord. On the other hand, they may be perceived as advantageous (e.g., new computer-ready spaces) and provide an improved space for future tenants. You can negotiate to have the landlord cover or share the costs of the work. If you pay for your part up front, it will cost you less, but if you need a loan to do so, it may be better to apply the costs to your monthly rent for the first few years of the term of your lease.

Ask about the current and potential future **uses of the building**. You will want to negotiate to exclude the landlord from signing any tenants who will be your competitors. For example, a chiropractor may choose to have in her lease the exclusion of other chiropractors, physiotherapists, massage therapists, and osteopaths as building tenants. If an important aspect of your service is to have a quiet, comforting, and relaxing atmosphere, businesses that generate noise may be a concern. On another front, you will need to know the limits of the **hours of operations** for the building. Tied into this is the issue of building security. When do the doors open and close? Are you able to get the flexibility you need in your lease? If you plan to have evening and weekend hours but this building functions as an 8 am to 6 pm, Monday to Friday office building, the landlord may not agree to change the hours due to the potential liability or the cost of security. Or, they may agree to be flexible but insist on passing on increased costs to you, the tenant.

TAKE HOME MESSAGE

Everything's negotiable.

Corollary:
Don't let them know you want it!

Signage is often another potential area for concern. What outside signage are you allowed to have? What inside signage and location identifiers are there? Can you have additional signage space or size? What will that cost you? If your clients can't find you, and if you cannot use signage effectively for marketing purposes, it may be that that particular location or landlord is not for you.

Looking at the next steps, you need to determine what options there will be for **renewing your lease** at the completion of your term. Investigate a renewal clause with a formula for calculating costs and a guarantee of right of first refusal to your own space when the lease expires. Include the length of time you have to exercise this right and ensure that they do not include an automatic renewal if you do not notify them of your intent to relocate. Similarly, you may wish to add a right of first refusal to any adjacent building spaces to give you the opportunity to expand if you wish. In addition, use your contract to protect you against the landlord declaring bankruptcy or selling the building, thereby voiding your lease. Ask for a "**non-disturbance**" clause that protects you against being evicted or being charged a significant increase in rent by a new owner or the bank.

Your own, trusted inspector should **inspect** the facilities. Bring in someone who will look at the communications wiring, the electrical systems and wiring, the plumbing, and the building and space construction. They will either give their seal of approval or make suggestions for needed upgrades. Those upgrades can then be recommended to the landlord. Make sure it is clear that without the important upgrades being made, you will not consider renting the space. Less vital, but yet desirable upgrades then become points of negotiation. It is also a good idea to look into the **building zoning**. Make sure the city planning office gives you the green light on operating your proposed current and future services in that location.

Having fun yet?

12.4 Let's Look at the Size and Design of Your Space

Here's where the real fun begins. Almost all of us like the chance to design the layout of our practice. Start with the services you are planning to offer. From this beginning will come what equipment, supplies, and furniture you will need. That in turn, leads to having an idea of what space you will need.

Tanis, a physiotherapist, and Boyd, a chiropractor, signed a partnership agreement to start a clinical practice offering their services, as well as massage therapy and podiatry. To do so, they devised a list of their requirements. That was the easy part. What they couldn't figure out was what space they should designate for each area of the clinic. As a solution, they each chatted with a few colleagues currently in a private clinic setting to get their advice. Treatment space seemed to be standard at approximately 7' x 10' for a cubicle and 10' x 10' for an assessment room. The rest was a free-for-all, so they guessed. After the first draft was done, they added up the total and decided they needed 2,480 square feet of space.

You can see from the above example that, just the act of putting this list together gave Tanis and Boyd a jump on linking their services to their capital needs (leaseholds, furnishings, and equipment). This will help immeasurably when they fill in their business plan's financial sections.

Having already looked at local real estate trends, this came to $3,472.00 a month for a "grossed-up" lease. This was a bit grander than they had planned so they reviewed the services, rooms, and space allotments and began cutting. They eliminated one washroom by getting official recognition of the public washroom on that floor of the building. In addition they decided the gym and open cubicle space would allow for group education classes and that they could downsize the storage room. This saved $738.14 a month, kept their core services intact, and allowed them to start designing the proposed site.

The first step for any new space is to take existing architectural drawings, copy them, and mark them up by hand, trying out several combinations of how the space might be divided. Remember that every time you take down or put up a new wall it will cost money. So, try to keep to the original design whenever feasible.

For each layout you consider, follow a "typical" client on the blueprint from the time they enter the clinic, to reception, assessment, treatment, and payment or rescheduling; see if the flow is efficient and avoids disrupting other clients and staff who are in the space at the same time. Is the layout optimal for patient safety? That is, are you able to see and hear anyone who needs you, and are all flow patterns free of obstacles? How will the noise level be? Is there sufficient privacy for taking a history or for providing personal financial information? Do the windows open into public spaces such as a kitchen or education space, or do they open into private spaces such as an assessment or treatment room? If the latter, you will have to add window coverings for privacy.

The following pages describe what 2,000 square feet might look like when it is partitioned off into the spaces Tanis and Boyd designated (Figure 12.1), and compare it to a sole proprietor, home office and treatment space (Figure 12.2).

In the end, once Tanis and Boyd had finished their layout, they had lost some space in a few rooms but they saved windows for the gym and administrative offices. This decision minimized the plumbing and wiring revisions, and left them with a fairly good client and staff flow (Figure 12.1).

The home office practitioner has chosen to incorporate the family's first floor washroom into the clinic and have the clients come in from the rear of the house to minimize any disruption to the neighbourhood (Figure 12.2). This clinician has realized the same efficiencies for plumbing as Tanis and Boyd by having those pieces adjacent to each other. Also, by ensuring their work desk is open and facing the waiting room, they are able to manage the client traffic themselves.

Once you have a "final" draft of your floor plan, check out the space for the appropriate computer and electrical wiring and outlets, telephone jacks, and lighting. The more spaces that have individually controlled lighting and reserve wiring, the easier it will be to create the ambiance and function you may need. Those will have to be factored in when making any physical changes and when estimating the costs of doing so. Remember to consider not only current needs but also your future needs. Also, consider the ease of wireless computer systems and concerns regarding client confidentiality – a few firewalls should allow for both. To avoid unanticipated costs after opening, it is a good idea to have your plans reviewed by an architect, or at minimum, a seasoned private practitioner and business owner. This help, along with your inspector's input as described earlier, may be invaluable, saving you huge headaches and costs in the future.

12.5 So, What did you Forget?

You may need one more kick at the can before signing off on the lease and the leaseholds. Take another look at the equipment and furniture items in your lists and your proposed personnel and services, and link them back to your clinic design. If there is a place for everything, then you are on your way. You won't know for sure, though, until you put your finances together. Hang on until Chapter 14 ("The Financial Plan: Starting and Ending Up Here") to complete the picture.

This is also a chance to return to your Vision Statement. Are you planning to expand? Are you hoping to have a contract with a local gym or another practitioner to share space, equipment, or staff? If you answer yes to any of these questions, is the location and design of your clinic designed to make the transition(s) viable and relatively simple?

TAKE HOME MESSAGE

It is not just a space, it is flow, function, and potential.

Corollary:
Check and recheck, and double check!

Table 12.1 Clinic Design Preparation – Linking Service to Space and Equipment Need

Service	# of Rooms	Room/Space Type	Equipment	Furniture	Space (sq. ft.)
Reception/Medical Record Storage	1	•open counter with sliding window •room and window locks •room for 2 staff to sit, 1 or 2 standing	•computer CPU, printer, monitor, mouse •telephone •safe	•counter •supplies cabinet •2 desk chairs •3 locking file cabinets	5' x 12'
Waiting	1	•open, adjacent to reception •children's play area •carpeted		•3 side tables •1 coffee table •12 chairs •small desk/cubicle •wall display units •coat rack/cupboard •children's toy box	10' x 10'
Toileting	2	•accessible washrooms (as mandated by zoning in this jurisdiction)	•hand paper towel wall units •2 toilets •2 sinks	•1 baby change table •1 chair	2 @ 8.2' x 8.2'
Client History and Assessment	2	•closed door	•BP cuff, stethoscope, dynamometer, goniometers, mobilization belt, X-ray viewer, reflex hammer, tuning fork, etc.	•small table •3chairs •1 plinth •1 rolling exam stool	2 @ 10' x 10'
Client Individual Treatment	7	•curtained •at least one fixed wall	•1 plinth	•1 small table/cabinet •1 foot stool •1 rolling exam stool	7 @ 7' x 10'
Exercise	1	•open •floor rubber matting	•6 aerobic pieces •1 universal gym •1 low mat •2 wall pulley set ups	•free weights •free weight stand •2 weight benches •2 small chart tables •1 equipment cabinet •2 display wall units	12' x 16'

Table 12.1 Continued

Room	Qty	Notes	Equipment	Furniture	Dimensions
Group Education	1	• closed door • carpeted • capacity for 22 persons	• data projector • screen • black board • DVD, video player, TV monitor • 2 AV carts	• 4 collapsible tables • 25 stackable chairs • 4 wall display units • 2 shelving units • 2 locking cabinets	20' x 20'
Staff Charting	1	• windows facing treatment areas • inaccessible to clients if locked • accommodates 6 staff, 2 students • carpeted	• 4 computer stations • 2 telephones with 2-lines total	• 8 individual carols • 8 desk chairs • 4 stackable chairs • 10 lockers	12' x 16'
Owner's Administration	1	• closed door • carpeted	• 2 computer systems	• 2 floor desks • 2 desk chairs • 2 lounge chairs • 1 coffee table • 1 cabinet • 2 floor-to-ceiling book shelves	12' x 16'
Laundry Equipment/ Supplies Storage	1	• for washing, drying, folding and storage of towels, linens, cleaning supplies, equipment • closed door	• stacking washer and dryer • vacuum • sink • modalities (US, interferential, acupuncture supplies, ice/hot packs, hydrocollator)	• folding counter • under counter cabinets • drying rack • above counter cabinets • broom closet	6' x 10'
Kitchen/ Lunchroom	1	• staff kitchen and lunch room	• microwave • coffee maker • tea kettle • toaster oven • fridge • sink	• 2 counters with cabinets • 1 table • 12 stackable chairs • garbage & recycling bins	10' x 16'
Hallways	2	• carpeted			2 @ 50' x 5'
TOTAL					**2,480**

(NB: Try Barrier-free Design Consultants: Betty Dion Enterprises Ltd. (www.bDel.ca); or Queen's University Accessibility Guidelines 1997© . Kingston: Queen's University (www.queensu.ca/camplan/reports/aguide/index.html), for the dimensions and designs of accessible, barrier-free spaces. Reference from Kathy Pringle.)

Figure 12.1 Multidisciplinary Clinic Layout

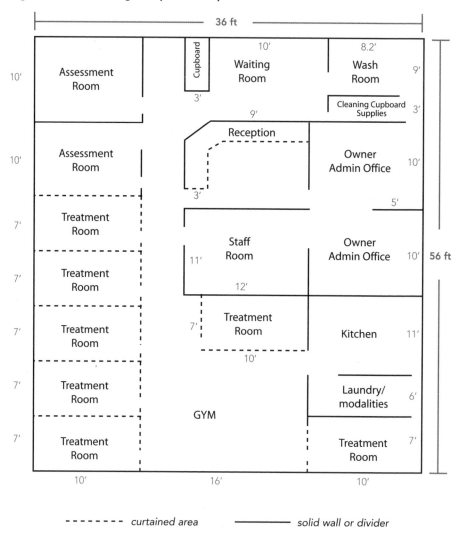

- - - - - - - - curtained area   ———— solid wall or divider

(Two curtained treatment areas and one assessment room/clinician, centralized administration space, and good client flow patterns optimize function.)

Figure 12.2 Single Practitioner Home Based Clinic Layout

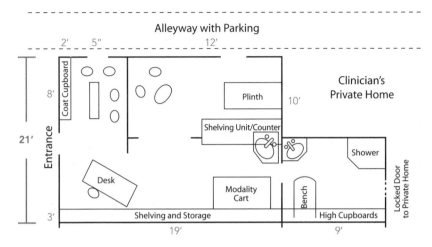

(The renovation of space within your home allows for significant cost savings and efficiencies. The location of the administrative space with direct sightlines to the waiting area, treatment space, washroom, and equipment storage spaces gives the sole practitioner more control and optimal efficiency.)

CHAPTER 13
Your Marketing Strategy: *How* to Make it Work
DIANA H. HOPKINS-ROSSEEL,DEC, BSC(PT), MSC(REHAB), MCPA

13.1 Marketing Fundamentals

Marketing is one of the most misunderstood aspects of small business. Yet, marketing is vital to all businesses and often means the difference between success and failure.

Marketing is defined as the means used to make a communication about a product or service, the purpose of which is to encourage recipients of the message to purchase or use the product or service.

Although many of us think of marketing as advertising, sales, and promotion, marketing is a much broader concept and set of activities and, most importantly, a process. Marketing includes research, product/service definition, product/service design and development, pricing, marketing strategy development, sales, advertising, distribution, and promotion.

At this point, you have already done the majority of your **research**. You have defined your consumers' needs, you have narrowed those needs to your target market(s) or niche(s), you have investigated your competition for prime opportunities, and you have selected your key services (and in some cases products). What is missing is the research on pricing: establishing the fees or prices you will charge for every component of the services you offer. Once these elements of your research are down to sufficient detail to allow you to move forward, you will take the last step to try and determine what advertising, sales, and promotions tactics have a history of being the most effective at reaching, influencing, and convincing your customers and referral sources to use your particular services or buy your products. For each of these steps you want to document not only what the answer is, but why. For instance, seniors prefer ground-floor practices due to anxieties related to access and poor mobility. When you know the why, you have the option of either locating your practice on the ground floor so as to service your customers' needs, or on another level, due to financial constraints. In the second case, you would then promote the easy access to your site via state-of-the-art electronic doorways and efficient elevators.

Once your research is in place, you complete the process of **defining and describing your products and/or services**. In order to promote those services, they will have to be described in lay terms for the public and, in some cases, your referral sources. If you cannot communicate what you do to your target audience easily, clearly, and succinctly they will not buy in. Remember, as a health care private practice owner and provider you are primarily selling services to your customers. These are the skills you have been educated and trained to provide. But as we provide those services we often find that there are products we would like to offer, usually because they are either difficult to source, local demand exceeds supplies, available products do not meet your standards or your customers' needs, or they are too costly for some of your customers. If you do opt to sell products, ensure that your adhere to the rules of your regulatory body and/or your provincial/territorial legislation in the sale of products, and that any potential conflict of interest has been identified, documented, and communicated to your clients.

TAKE HOME MESSAGE

Good market research breeds success.

Corollary: Target your efforts to your key audience.

Once you have a clear idea of the services you plan to offer, you will need to attach a price, or fee, to each individual component and/or product. The factors that influence pricing are:

1. competitors' prices;

2. current and anticipated supply and demand levels;

3. level of expertise and/or education required to perform that skill;

4. cost of providing the service; and

5. your pricing strategy (e.g., is the price set low in order to engage the customer and increase volumes, moderately to be competitive, or high to communicate excellence or unique value?).

Finally we come to the **marketing strategy**. A strategy is a plan for achieving goals. A marketing strategy is a plan to increase or maintain your percentage of the market. The 2 major marketing strategies used in practice are characterized as the "Push Strategy" and the "Pull Strategy." The *Push Strategy* is designed to make the customer aware of the service.

If a family physician has free prescription pads for your services on the desk in his/her office, they are more likely to remember you exist, and are more likely to prescribe your services. Similarly, if you provide all local relevant specialists and family physicians with a monthly newsletter and waiting room pamphlets with valid information on the newest research in your area and theirs, and on health tips for their patients, your clinic's presence in the environment may push them to consider your services. In retail businesses, the push strategy is the method of convincing the retailer to carry your product. It is then the retailer who gets the product to the consumer. The **Pull Strategy** works to increase consumer demand directly. If you are able to convince potential clients that they need your services for pain relief, they will demand referrals from their physician or insurance provider, or they will seek out your services directly. Advertising and promotion are often cornerstones of this strategy. Providing public lectures on pain relief at the local library will often result in immediate demand by audience members asking for your business card, or in the future when they visit their physician with complaints of pain.

You can use the push strategy alone and successfully promote some products or services. For instance, most people do not differentiate between brands of elastic resistance bands or practitioners of acupuncture. In these cases, therefore, it makes more sense to get your resistance bands on the clinicians' and retailers' shelves, and make your acupuncture skills known and respected by referral sources. On the other hand, marketers will tell you that you cannot use the pull strategy alone; it is always used with a push strategy. You are unlikely to want to spend the time or money on promoting your services to the public without ensuring that the primary referral sources are ready and willing to access your services for their patients. Take the example of the individual who has just undergone heart surgery and is ready to go home. Even though their best friend went to a cardiac rehabilitation centre after their surgery and they raved about it, and the patient asks their nurse about it, if the clinical staff in the hospital, their cardiologist, or their family physician do not make the referral, the patient is unlikely to pursue it further.

So, what are our options? Here's where we can bring in the **four "Ps" of marketing:** product, price, place, and promotion. And this leads us back to the *product*. You have already outlined your sustainable competitive advantages, including perhaps serving a unique niche (e.g., the under-serviced group of individuals with vestibular deficits). In addition, you will work hard to create customer loyalty through excellence and caring services. You may also have a unique service (e.g., you are the only clinic in the area with vocational rehabilitation services). To these sustainable advantages for your product you then need to provide *non-sustainable competitive advantages*. Marketers will say that without these, you won't have a business. These strategies will have to be fluid, changing with the trends in supply and demand, consumer types, and economic and political shifts. Advertising can provide a temporary competitive advantage but it is by its very nature non-sustainable. This is also true of perceptions of quality – your clients may have gravitated towards new machines and modalities in the past but are now seeking individual hands-on care. This is often termed "sensory marketing." The design features of your business are another non-sustainable device to derive a competitive advantage. If you provide invasive health care services, your customers may be looking for a white, crisp, sterile environment; on the other hand, those providing stress reduction and relaxation services may have to design a quiet, subdued environment to satisfy their customers. These consumer perceptions and their responses should be monitored for change over time.

The second of the four "Ps" is *price*. As outlined above, the prices you set – although not the only factor – are directly linked to client interest and satisfaction. Practically speaking, prices must be set high enough to ensure that the business is solvent, breaking even at minimum and making a profit in the end. Price a service too high and you may price yourself out of the market; too low and you may devalue your services or not meet your bottom line. A key element to pricing professional services, which is often ignored or forgotten, is the impact it has on payer groups and the overall incomes of the members of your profession. If you price your services low for individuals who are having difficulty paying, insurance providers are unlikely to pay more for the same service. If you and your competitors continue to cut your prices to try to gain an advantage, you may all lose in the end. If you are not able to be transparent, and demonstrate the cost of doing business and communicate those costs to the public and all payers, they are likely to see your services as overpriced.

Sabina and Nathan are personal trainers who provide services in local fitness facilities and in individual client's homes. The cost of the initial assessment and program development is $100.00. Each subsequent training session is $45.00 or $90.00 for three sessions/week. The majority of clients used the training sessions regularly for three months and then only a couple of times a year for a review and revision of their program. This means that an average client would have services totalling $1,180.00. Right from the start-up of this business, Sabina and Nathan had agreed to provide a sliding fee scale, including some pro bono services to those who could not afford their regular fees to give something back to the community. They had no expertise or interest in reviewing individual's finances; they took it at face value that other professionals had already made that determination and waited for them to refer these clients to them. Unfortunately, by the end of their first year in business they had to rescind all offers of reduced fees. What they discovered was that the majority of the clients referred to them for reduced fees of $560.00 or less, had, in that same period, purchased exercise equipment or other leisure items (such as a large-screen TV) for values equivalent to or exceeding the amount they had been excused from paying.

In this scenario there are two issues of concern. The first is to evaluate the risk/benefit ratio of giving away the control of your income to an outside body. Having other professionals – who would not suffer financial repercussions from reduced fees – generate these, decreased their administrative tasks but also gave away ownership of the process; as a result, Sabina and Nathan suffered financial losses. The second follows from the first: if you make a decision about your fees, you must also develop the policies and procedures to support that decision. They could have set very specific criteria for including or excluding someone applying for consideration from receiving a reduction in fees. That may take some extra time but it would also preclude the unanticipated misuse of the provision.

The third "P" of marketing is *place*, which refers to how you get your product to your customer. In the case of health care services, you may break this down into the location where the services are provided. Is it a *destination location*, where the

TAKE HOME MESSAGE

There is more to marketing than meets the eye.

Corollary:
Make it simple,
make a plan.

customer goes where the service is provided? If you have a unique service or are know to be the best in your area, your clients will come to you. If you previously developed significant customer loyalty at your first practice, your current customers will often disadvantage themselves to stay with you, and move with you to your new location. Or is it an *impulse location*, where getting individuals to the service is more traffic dependent? Use dentists, optometrists, and chiropractors as examples. You may have noticed that in the last decade or so there are more and more of these professionals locating their services within shopping malls. Similarly, many health care professionals locate in "medical" buildings where multiple health care practitioners have clinics and many refer to each other. They are doing so because they know the individuals using that location for other products or services are more likely to choose their clinic when their type of services are required. In the case of selling goods, it can be as straightforward as which shelf to place the item on, or as complex as what retailers or wholesalers to promote the item to.

The final "P" is **promotion**. Promotion is how you let people know what you've got for sale. It includes most of the things you think of when "marketing" is mentioned including, but not limited to, advertising, sales promotion, and publicity. Your choice of push and/or pull strategy will start to direct your efforts. But let's take a cursory look at the variety and breadth of options available to you as a business owner. *Advertising* is used to get a potential customer to try a product for the first time. The means of advertising may be divided into three categories: 1) directly to individuals' homes in the form of mailings, the Internet, and telemarketing; 2) in the public arena on billboards, buses, subways, and entertainment or shopping venues; or 3) the media, including radio, television, newspapers, and magazines. Each of these methods has advantages and disadvantages. To choose you must investigate cost (TV ads are often beyond your reach), quality, longevity (newspaper ads are short lived), interactivity (the Internet can be highly responsive), exposure to the competition (public arena ads will be seen by your competition), attention of the receiver (radio often does not have the listener's full attention), audience base (TV reaches a wide audience, magazines reach a target audience), and consumer value (giving a public lecture is highly appreciated by the select audience). *Sales promotion* actually takes it a step further and encourages potential consumers to buy into a product using incentives. In the case of goods, we have all experienced promotional sales, coupons, contests, and free samples for example. Sales promotion of services is similar. Take the chiropractor who sets up a booth in a mall or during a special event, and offers a free spinal assessment; or an orthotist who demonstrates how foot molds and orthotics are made. *Publicity*, or public relations, is also considered promotion. It is free publicity if your clinic is mentioned in the local paper or your profession is mentioned in the national paper in a news piece. It is good public relations if you organize a local charity event.

In the end, the marketing of your business is only as good as your analysis of its effectiveness. For every marketing device you put in place, you must have a way to evaluate the outcomes. When a client first comes to you, have standardized and documented methods for finding out how they came to you: physician referral (if so, who?), advertising (if so, which one?), word of mouth or reputation (if so, who promoted the clinic?). Both during a long-term client's time at the clinic and at discharge for all clients, ask them to complete a "client satisfaction survey." There are many validated surveys that you may select from. Then, on a regular basis, review all the data you have collected and make decisions regarding ongoing and future marketing. If 90% of your referrals are due to word of mouth and previous clients' high levels of satisfaction, perhaps you may cease any advertising. If, on the other hand, 90% of your referrals are from local health care practitioners, you may want to maintain your marketing directed at those sources and change your marketing to the public to diversify your sources of new clients.

13.1.1 How do I Know How much Money I should Allocate to my Marketing Plan?

In the for-profit world, it's fairly standard to determine a marketing budget by allocating 10–20% of projected gross revenues to marketing and communications. In other words, use the figure that reflects your revenues before taxes and expenditures are subtracted to calculate how much you should spend. Despite lower revenues in the early years of the business, it is often recommended that your percentage allocated to marketing be higher. The other side of the coin is that you must work to avoid a deficit budget.

Seth and Cindy both opened orthopaedic physiotherapy clinics with equivalent operating costs. Prior to start-up, Seth projected cash receipts totalling $125,958.00 in the first year and allocated $8,150.00 to marketing, or 6.47%. Cindy projected cash receipts totalling $201,863.00 in the first year and allotted $7,757.00 to marketing, or 3.84%. At the end of the first year, Seth had made a net profit of $14,900.00, while Cindy saw $1,200.00 profit. In the second year, Seth decreased his marketing budget to 4.16% of projected receipts but this actually came to $10,800.00. Due to her tight bottom line in year 1, Cindy decreased her marketing allotment in year 2 to 1.96% of projected gross revenues, or $6,480.00. Seth saw a net profit of $40,900.00 while Cindy had a net profit of $25,200.00.

Without extensive analysis, there is no way to determine if there was a direct relationship between Seth and Cindy's marketing budgets, and their profits. Marketing researchers tell us however, that putting less than 6–8% of projected gross revenues towards marketing and communication does have a negative impact on most small business earnings.

TAKE HOME MESSAGE

Marketing your business is not a luxury.

Corollary:
Let them know you are there, they will find out you care.

If you are working on a very tight budget and do not feel you have the funds to increase your marketing portion, substitute or increase those marketing methods that you cannot see in your spreadsheets because they do not require an outlay of funds. For instance, you can do volunteer work in the community using your professional title or skills, or enhance the atmosphere of your clinic with improving staff attitudes, or add background music to differentiate and promote your business. Just remember that YOUR TIME IS VALUABLE and any work paid for "in kind" must not be considered worthless or discounted when looking at the cost of doing business.

13.2 The Fundamentals in Practice

A beginning note of caution when embarking on any marketing plan: you must check your professional regulations and legislation to ensure that you are not in breach of those rules, thereby risking sanctions, including possible suspension or loss of your professional registration.

In addition, a good rule of thumb is to use a variety of marketing methods and tools both to help build a wide client base, as well as to give you the opportunity to evaluate which ones are most effective at engaging and retaining clients.

Giselle is a physiotherapist whose primary service is general orthopaedics. Samantha is a sports physiotherapist who works with national professional teams and has a part-time private sports clinic. Angelo is an occupational therapist who sells motivational and counselling videos, audiotapes, and DVDs as well as offering counselling services to individuals with vocational needs. Madeline is an audiologist providing testing services in paediatrics and runs continuing education courses in audiology for audiologists, speech language pathologists, and Ear, Nose and Throat (ENT) physicians across the country.

Each one of these practices is likely to have a very different and distinct approach to marketing because they offer unique services, provided in a variety of venues to dissimilar audiences.

Giselle, as a sole practitioner with no spare time or discretionary funds to speak of, chose to focus most of her marketing efforts on customer loyalty through excellent service. She made sure she delivered on her Mission Statement by providing services on time, in a congenial atmosphere, with obvious enthusiasm, and based on current best practices. She measured and documented treatment outcomes regularly and made changes in approach when indicated, to promote efficient and effective therapy. In line with this strategy, she made sure to take the time to communicate by phone and in writing with all her referral sources. She also made sure she had strict, transparent policies on methods of fee payment. Finally, she requested her client satisfaction survey be completed anonymously by all clients, and directed her clients to use the comments box available whenever they had a comment or concern.

Samantha, although also dedicated to excellence in care, put her marketing time and funds into supporting one local high school football team and one summer community soccer team. She provided them with funding for their uniforms and equipment purchases, as well as being present whenever she could at their home games to be their volunteer trainer. In addition, in the case of the soccer team, her clinic name appeared on their team shirt-sleeves and on one of their community trophies. In return she was visible, her skills were recognized as effective, and she gained the goodwill of the community.

Angelo's task was more daunting. On the surface it looked as if he had a built-in customer base for his tapes and DVDs in his counselling clients. In fact, he knew he could be perceived as being in a direct conflict of interest if his clients felt that, due to their therapeutic relationship, they should purchase these goods. His solution was twofold: first he directed most of his tape and DVD marketing efforts to direct Internet sales. Second, he provided every client, and, if appropriate, their insurance provider, with a verbal and written explanation of their options, including that there was no requirement for such products for the client to receive effective care and an alphabetized list of similar products they could purchase elsewhere. The documentation made it clear to the clients that he would be making a profit on the sale of any of the items. He took a completely different approach to marketing his counselling services. He directed the majority of his time and money at large- and medium-sized institutions, where the economics of lost days from work due to injury or illness would be a priority. His approach was to do extensive research into the cost of lost days, and the cost and effectiveness of vocational counselling. Armed with this information, he produced a succinct report and audiovisuals for potential client companies. Then he put his suit and tie on, and argued his case to the management of those companies.

TAKE HOME MESSAGE

Take the time to know which of your marketing strategies worked and which didn't.

Corollary: What worked before may not now; keep checking.

Madeline first set up her practice because of the long waiting list for her services in the public sector. She realized very quickly in private practice that a percentage of potential clients would prefer to, or have to, stay on a waiting list for publicly-covered services rather than pay for expedited testing. She decided to market to daycare workers, teachers, and parents, with easily interpreted pamphlets on the benefits of early testing intervention. Her second method was to present her services to physicians at their monthly association and departmental meetings. Within a week of those meetings she would contact each of the physicians who attended by phone or by sending out an information pamphlet and referral forms to their offices. Initial funding of the development of her course curricula was from her own pocket. She then advertised in each profession's association newsletter and on their Web site. These ads were relatively inexpensive and specifically targeted the intended audience.

Ultimately, it all comes back to your market research; it will tell you whom you need to reach. Then, using your available budget and a predetermined timeline, develop a plan that fits, one that is feasible and equipped with measurable outcomes.

What not to do? Avoid mimicking the approach of others in your field until you somehow investigate their effectiveness. The practice across town may have mugs, pens, and fridge magnets with their clinic name on them but marketing and communications experts may be saying that the method is no longer novel, and is less effective than it used to be. Ask yourself, how many t-shirts can any one individual wear? You may see a competitor's ad in the Yellow Pages but find the cost prohibitive. Next time you are at a course or professional meeting, ask the private practitioners if they have used the Yellow Pages ads and if this method has worked for them. Request that every client answer a very short questionnaire at their first intake session, indicating how they heard about your services and who referred them to you. Add a voluntary client satisfaction survey after they have been discharged from your services to round out your information-gathering exercise on what the client's perceptions are on your effectiveness, and on the convenience, staff-client rapport, and efficiency of your services.

CHAPTER 14
The Financial Plan: Starting and Ending Up Here
DIANA H. HOPKINS-ROSSEEL,DEC, BSC(PT), MSC(REHAB), MCPA

14.1 The Basics

This is the point at which many health care practitioners' eyes glaze over with anticipated boredom, or the hairs rise on the back of their necks with the anxiety of entering unknown territory! Yet, recognizing that you may be ignorant in business financing and accounting, and that you lack experience is a great start.

We have all been told that we must be accountable – to our families, our clients, the government, and many others – in many areas of our lives. What does this mean? The definition of "accountable" could be said to be "to provide an account of," meaning you need to account for your actions. This is where your bookkeeping and financial statements come in. It is your opportunity to provide yourself and other stakeholders with a clear, interpretable picture of where the money came from and where it went. Only when you see the raw numbers do you have an unambiguous picture of your business' current status and future potential. The numbers will be your measuring stick. It is like vacuuming a filthy rug: seeing the clear path you create is very satisfying!

Here are a few definitions to get you started …

Accounting is the process of recording, analyzing, and interpreting the financial activities of a business. Regardless of the size or type of business, all businesses follow the same basic accounting procedures. This type of record keeping is also used for budgeting, or forecasting the income and expenditures of a business for the coming year. At the end of the year, the budget is compared to actual revenues and costs. The results allow the business to revise its operations to minimize expenditures and maximize income, thereby improving the balance. Then it starts all over again for the next year with budget projections of the next year's financial activities.

TAKE HOME MESSAGE
Don't be wary of business finance and accounting; you can do it.

Corollary:
Good accounting leads to peace of mind.

Bookkeeping is the fundamental day-to-day function of recording all transactions for a business in a specific format. Bookkeepers keep track of all transactions, from invoicing (billing) through payment. With the advent of the electronic era and e-commerce, a company's "books" are more often electronic, with the bookkeeping being performed using software databases. This information is then translated into financial statements.

Financial statements are the reports you create to summarize the financial performance of your business. Normally, businesses prepare three financial statements: 1) the balance sheet; 2) the income statement; and 3) the cash flow statement.

It is generally thought that service businesses, such as those delivering health care, require the simplest type of accounting. Compare selling the two main products of assessment and treatment (or a single product such as consulting), with an additional related product (e.g., the peripheral service of medico-legal reports), to a retail business, which sells 1,500 differently priced, stored, displayed, and distributed items! The absence of inventory, then, is the main difference.

14.2 The Template

Enclosed with this book is a CD-ROM with Microsoft Excel templates of the three financial statements noted above: the income statement, the balance sheet, and the cash flow statement. In addition, we have included the spreadsheets you will use to calculate the amounts that will eventually end up in the financial statements templates (Edmonds, Schell, Hopkins-Rosseel, 2007). These were developed in a business course for physiotherapists and occupational therapists when we discovered that it was very difficult to use the standard templates widely available because of their orientation to businesses that primarily sell goods rather than services; these templates did not allow for the detailed background data gathering and recording necessary to determine the pricing or fees for services offered.

The first, or main CD template, assumes your business bills almost exclusively for services rendered but does accommodate for sales of a small number of items. The second, the "Cost of Goods Sold" (COGS) CD template, assumes that the sale of goods (one item or more) is projected to be a significant percentage of your business revenues. If you remember back to the businesses discussed in Chapter 13, only Angelo's would use the COGS CD spreadsheets.

The purpose of these spreadsheets is to make everything easy for you. When you add a new number, or change an existing one, the software will automatically revise the calculations and provide new totals. All the sheets are linked so that the changes will travel through any relevant ones and end up in your three main financial reports.

14.3 Notes and Assumptions

Now you are down to actually putting some numbers into your spreadsheets. First, you will put a sub-section in your business plan in the financial section entitled "Notes and Assumptions to the Financials." Here you will clarify where your numbers are coming from. For instance, if you are entering numbers into your "Operating Expenses" spreadsheet in the "Licenses and Permits" column (see below), you will outline in your business plan what is included in that number. For example:

Start-Up Name Registration	$ 80.00		
Business License	$256.00		
Incorporation	$360.00		
Building Inspection	$150.00	**Total**	**$846.00**
Annual License	$160.00		

Only the total of $846.00 will appear in your Year 1 spreadsheet (see table 14.1 below). It is in the "Notes and Assumptions" section within the text of your plan that the breakdown is included. That way, there is always a detailed account of where you got the data from and how you calculated the numbers. You may add one or two sentences to clarify or remind yourself, or the reader, why any item is there or how to source it. For instance, you may put in the government Web site or contact information for business licenses or the rules of incorporation here for future reference. It also allows for easier business evaluation and revisions in the future. Another option is to append these notes and assumptions to the bottom of each spreadsheet rather than in a sub-section of the text.

You will use the "Revenue" spreadsheet to itemize your anticipated sources of income before your business gets underway, and while you are planning and preparing your business plan. Similarly, you will enter any projected costs in the remaining spreadsheets (e.g., Supplies, Assets, Banking, Utilities, Operating, Wages, and Marketing). These working spreadsheets are considered a component of the "Assumptions" piece of the plan. For this reason, you will incorporate them under that heading in a business plan. An alternative would be to include these spreadsheets in the appendices to the plan as background information. This latter method helps to keep the plan short and manageable. Either way, they are an essential and pivotal piece of the developing puzzle.

Table 14.1 Year 1: Operating Expenses

Year 1: Operating Expenses							
Month	Supplies	Licences and Permits	Cleaning Services	Leased Equipment	Accounting	Lawyer	Total Monthly
January	$	$ 846.00	$	$	$	$	$
February	$	$ 0.00	$	$	$	$	$
March	$	$ 0.00	$	$	$	$	$
April	$	$ 0.00	$	$	$	$	$
May	$	$ 0.00	$	$	$	$	$
June	$	$ 0.00	$	$	$	$	$
July	$	$ 0.00	$	$	$	$	$
August	$	$ 0.00	$	$	$	$	$
September	$	$ 0.00	$	$	$	$	$
October	$	$ 0.00	$	$	$	$	$
November	$	$ 0.00	$	$	$	$	$
December	$	$ 0.00	$	$	$	$	$
Total	$	$ 846.00	$	$	$	$	$

Remember that, as discussed above, for the majority of items you should have a short written statement to note the source(s) of, and/or rationale for, your projections. For example, make sure you note if your fees for your various services are based on an increment of time (e.g., $35.00/15 minute unit) or the actual service regardless of duration (e.g., assessments at $75.00 or group education sessions at $12.00/person). These written notes and assumptions also allow you to give a rationale for your projections. An example would be to note that you have decreased the numbers of clients you project serving in July, August, and December in anticipation of peak holiday periods.

Once you have made all of your projections by entering the numbers in the spreadsheets, the software program will do the calculations for you. This includes not only subtotals and totals for that individual sheet but also transfers the relevant data into the balance sheet, income statement, and cash flow spreadsheets. Throughout the process you should be checking these outcomes. If your projected business costs exceed revenues, you will have to rework your plans to cut costs, increase revenues, or both. This manipulation of the individual items is part of the strategy you use to do your planning, and to ensure the business will be feasible and that financing is sufficient. Therefore, don't be afraid to rework your plans and the corresponding numbers several times until they work, and the plan is comprehensive and cohesive.

Let's do a little calculating to see how this works. Let's say you decide to open "XX Clinic" starting with four products: psychometric testing (batteries of quality of life, coping and symptom inventories), clinical assessments, treatments, and medico-legal reports. The next step is to price the products. Then you project the numbers of each that will be billed each month. At this point your income may look quite impressive. Given the following assumptions, the annual income before costs would be projected at $276,720.

Assumptions:
1 clinician
5 psychometric testing sessions/week on Fridays
2 clinical assessments/day (approx 1 hour/assessment)
4 treatment sessions/hour, 6 hours/day, 4 days/week ($40.00 per treatment)
2 medico-legal reports/ month ($100.00/ page, avg. $150.00/ report)

Table 14.2 Year 1: Revenue Assumptions

Year 1: Revenue Assumptions

Month	Psychometric Testing			Clinical Assessment			Treatment			Reports			Total Monthly Billings
	Clients	Price	Total	Clients	Price	Total	Clients	Price	Total	Clients	Price	Total	
Jan	20	$250	$5,000	32	$75	$2,400	384	$40	$15,360	2	$150	$300	$23,060
Feb	20	$250	$5,000	32	$75	$2,400	384	$40	$15,360	2	$150	$300	$23,060
Mar	20	$250	$5,000	32	$75	$2,400	384	$40	$15,360	2	$150	$300	$23,060
April	20	$250	$5,000	32	$75	$2,400	384	$40	$15,360	2	$150	$300	$23,060
May	20	$250	$5,000	32	$75	$2,400	384	$40	$15,360	2	$150	$300	$23,060
June	20	$250	$5,000	32	$75	$2,400	384	$40	$15,360	2	$150	$300	$23,060
July	20	$250	$5,000	32	$75	$2,400	384	$40	$15,360	2	$150	$300	$23,060
Aug	20	$250	$5,000	32	$75	$2,400	384	$40	$15,360	2	$150	$300	$23,060
Sept	20	$250	$5,000	32	$75	$2,400	384	$40	$15,360	2	$150	$300	$23,060
Oct	20	$250	$5,000	32	$75	$2,400	384	$40	$15,360	2	$150	$300	$23,060
Nov	20	$250	$5,000	32	$75	$2,400	384	$40	$15,360	2	$150	$300	$23,060
Dec	20	$250	$5,000	32	$75	$2,400	384	$40	$15,360	2	$150	$300	$23,060
TOTAL			$60,000			$28,800			$184,320			$3,600	$276,720

Now, before looking at the costs of providing these services, could you pick out some problems with these projections? Consider the following "reality checks":

1. Have you accounted for days away from work due to illness, professional development activities, family sick days, bereavement days, and vacations?

2. Is there a way to incorporate "no shows" and other causes of decreased productivity?

3. What happens if you are not able to start providing services on opening day due to unanticipated delays?

4. What if your referral rate is slow in your initial months of practice?

5. Did you account for natural variations in attendance rates (e.g., will it be slower in the summer or during flu season)?

Try expanding your assumptions to account for these variations:
Addendum:
10   professional development days/year
12   sick days/year
9   statutory holiday days/year
10   vacation days/year (= 218 working days; 44 weeks/year)
0   clients in month 1
↑   clientele slowly over months 2 and 3
3   treatments/hour
↓   clientele July, August, and December

Therefore, a more realistic picture of your potential income in year 1 might look like that depicted in table 14.3.

Table 14.3 Year 1: Revised Revenue Assumptions

Month	Psychometric Testing			Clinical Assessment			Treatment			Reports			Total Monthly Billings
	Clients	Price	Total	Clients	Price	Total	Clients	Price	Total	Clients	Price	Total	
Jan	0	$250	$-	0	$75	$-	0	$40	$-	0	$150	$-	$-
Feb	4	$250	$1,000	9	$75	$675	0	$40	$-	1	$150	$150	$1,825
Mar	12	$250	$3,000	20	$75	$1,500	0	$40	$-	2	$150	$300	$4,800
April	20	$250	$5,000	28	$75	$2,100	215	$40	$8,600	2	$150	$300	$16,000
May	20	$250	$5,000	28	$75	$2,100	215	$40	$8,600	2	$150	$300	$16,000
June	20	$250	$5,000	28	$75	$2,100	215	$40	$8,600	2	$150	$300	$16,000
July	4	$250	$1,000	18	$75	$1,350	145	$40	$5,800	0	$150	$-	$8,150
Aug	8	$250	$2,000	22	$75	$1,650	168	$40	$6,720	1	$150	$150	$10,520
Sept	20	$250	$5,000	28	$75	$2,100	215	$40	$8,600	2	$150	$300	$16,000
Oct	20	$250	$5,000	28	$75	$2,100	215	$40	$8,600	2	$150	$300	$16,000
Nov	20	$250	$5,000	28	$75	$2,100	215	$40	$8,600	2	$150	$300	$16,000
Dec	10	$250	$-	20	$75	$1,500	145	$40	$5,800	1	$150	$150	$7,450
TOTAL	158		$37,000			$19,275			$69,920			$2,550	$128,745

The optimistic – and we would suggest overestimated – projection for "XX Clinic" of $276,720.00 has become the more realistic amount of $128,745.00. This revised income may or may not appear sufficient. Before rethinking your fees or another component of revenues (such as your hours of work), take the next step: calculate your costs.

When projecting your costs, the more detailed you get, the more accurate you are; the more comprehensive you are, the more likely it will be that you do not underestimate your costs. The type of business you plan to open will dictate your costs and, therefore, what spreadsheets you will require. The spreadsheet templates we have provided allow you to itemize your anticipated costs in great detail. For example, you can list and cost office supplies and/or clinic supplies right down to a box of tissues. The combined monthly sum of these two then appears in the Operating Expenses spreadsheet. Finally, the monthly totals calculated in the Operating Expenses are transferred to the Cash Flow Statement for that year. These last two steps are performed by the Excel program and do not require you to input any figures! Even better than that, if you change even a single item in the supplies list, the program will revise the totals and each of the other spreadsheets almost simultaneously.

The same process happens when you enter your "assets" into the spreadsheets. In accounting, **Assets** are defined as "the entire property of a person, association, corporation, or estate applicable or subject to the payment of debts." The total assets of your business will be calculated by the Excel program and appear on the Balance Sheet. The assets entered into the **Fixed Assets** spreadsheet in our program, on the other hand, are defined more narrowly as "equipment, furniture, buildings, etc., which are purchased and used for long-term purposes." This spreadsheet is broken down into the "non-capital" and "capital" categories. Capital assets are those that are considered of substantial worth in the context of that particular business. Each business (or industry) will define the level at which items are considered part of the capital assets of the business. For our purposes, you may stipulate that all items of $500.00 or more are capital assets. Some clinics or businesses may prefer a value of $1,000.00. A way to determine the cut-off value is to ask the question: "At what price would an item we own be difficult to sell quickly?"

In the example below, "XX Clinic" has started with projected operating expenses of $9,272.00 and assets of $21,707.00 ($15,356.00 plus $6,351.00). The total of **$30,979.00** then looks reasonable with an income of **$128,745.00**. So what's missing?

Table 14.4 Year 1: Office Supplies

Year 1: Office Supplies			
Item	**Quantity**	**Price**	**Total**
Appointment Cards (100/pkg)	8	$5.00	**$40.00**
Client Manila File Folders (50/pkg)	16	$7.00	**$112.00**
Paper (5000 sheets)	4	$60.00	**$240.00**
Pens (12/box)	12	$5.00	**$60.00**
Pencils (12/box)	4	$3.00	**$12.00**
Highlighters (12/box)	2	$6.00	**$12.00**
Self-stick Notes (12/pack)	6	$4.00	**$24.00**
Envelopes (500/box)	5	$15.00	**$75.00**
2" Binders	20	$4.00	**$80.00**
Rubber Bands (100/box)	2	$3.00	**$6.00**
Paper Clips (1000/box)	1	$2.00	**$2.00**
Staples (2500/box)	2	$4.00	**$8.00**
First Aid Kit	1	$75.00	**$75.00**
Ink cartridges	12	$70.00	**$840.00**
Tissues (10 small boxes/unit)	5	$5.00	**$25.00**
Educational Books	8	$85.00	**$680.00**
Anatomical Models	2	$150.00	**$300.00**
Educational Videos, DVDs	4	$22.00	**$88.00**
Magazine Subscriptions	2	$25.00	**$50.00**
Toys	5	$8.00	**$40.00**
Other	0	$ -	**$-**
TOTAL			**$2,769.00**
Purchased Every 6 Months			**$1,384.50**

Table 14.5 Year One: Clinical Supplies

Year 1: Clinical Supplies			
Item	Quantity	Price	Total
Quality of Life Tool	1	$150.00	$150.00
Symptom Inventory	1	$150.00	$150.00
Coping Strategies Inventory	1	$250.00	$250.00
Motor Dexterity Kit	1	$275.00	$275.00
Latex-free Gloves (100/box)	5	$11.00	$55.00
Medical Tape (10/box)	4	$18.00	$72.00
Assessment Gowns	10	$9.00	$90.00
Face Cloths	50	$2.00	$100.00
Towels	100	$4.00	$400.00
Massage Oil (1 litre/unit)	6	$32.00	$192.00
Timers	6	$3.00	$18.00
Soap (liquid) (1 litre/unit)	24	$6.00	$144.00
Hand Sanitizer (150 ml/unit)	12	$12.00	$144.00
Paper Towels (18 rolls)	3	$28.00	$84.00
Toilet Paper (45 rolls)	5	$15.00	$75.00
Cleaning Cloths (10/box)	25	$5.00	$125.00
Cleaning Solution (1 litre/unit)	10	$15.00	$150.00
Pillow Cases	20	$6.00	$120.00
Sheets	50	$8.00	$400.00
Hand Putty (5 strengths)	4	$38.00	$152.00
Electrode Gel	15	$15.00	$225.00
Other	0	$ -	$ -
TOTAL			$3,371.00
Purchased Every 3 Months			$842.75

Table 14.6 Non-Capital Assets

Non-Capital Assets (Value Less than $500)			
Fixed Assets	**Quantity**	**Price**	**Total**
Front Desk	1	$300.00	**$300.00**
Clinician Desk	1	$200.00	**$200.00**
Clinic Chairs	5	$110.00	**$550.00**
Ergonomic Admin. Office Chairs	2	$100.00	**$200.00**
Bookshelves	4	$120.00	**$480.00**
Office Chairs (stacking)	20	$16.00	**$320.00**
Client Filing Cabinet with Locks (4-drawer)	2	$60.00	**$120.00**
Waiting Room Chairs	6	$25.00	**$150.00**
Electronic Cash Register	1	$125.00	**$125.00**
Ergonomic Gel Wrist Rests	2	$4.00	**$8.00**
All-in-one Laser Printer (with fax)	1	$150.00	**$150.00**
Dot Matrix Colour Printer	1	$60.00	**$60.00**
Front Desk Telephone with Headset	1	$80.00	**$80.00**
Clinician Telephone	1	$60.00	**$60.00**
Paper Shredder	1	$50.00	**$50.00**
Floor Exercise Mats (Airex)	5	$290.00	**$1,450.00**
Exercise Balls (3 heavy duty) (sm, med, lg)	1	$431.00	**$431.00**
Exercise Ball Storage Unit	1	$99.00	**$99.00**
Balance Board	1	$73.00	**$73.00**
Vertical Mirror (portable)	1	$180.00	**$180.00**
Television	1	$100.00	**$100.00**
VCR	1	$65.00	**$65.00**
DVD Player	1	$85.00	**$85.00**
Microwave	1	$120.00	**$120.00**
Coffee Maker	1	$25.00	**$25.00**
Student Desks	1	$150.00	**$150.00**
Student Chairs	1	$45.00	**$45.00**
Anatomical Models	3	$45.00	**$135.00**
Wall Posters	5	$25.00	**$125.00**
Pillows (clinic)	15	$12.00	**$180.00**
Wastebaskets	5	$8.00	**$40.00**
Storage File Cabinet for Inactive Files	2	$60.00	**$120.00**
Clock	3	$25.00	**$75.00**
Other	0	$-	**$-**
TOTAL			**$6,351.00**

Table 14.7 Capital Equipment – Purchased

Capital Equipment – Purchased			
Equipment	Quantity	Price	Total
TENS Machine	4	$240.00	$960.00
Wall-Mounted Low Mat Table	1	$995.00	$995.00
Biofeedback Machine	4	$310.00	$1,240.00
Clinic Treatment Table	1	$960.00	$960.00
Computer	2	$1,300.00	$2,600.00
Computer Software (pt mgmt, accounting, sensorimotor)	3	$500.00	$1,500.00
Refrigerator	1	$750.00	$750.00
Other	0	$ -	$-
TOTAL			$9,005.00
Asset Purchases			$15,356.00

Table 14.8 Capital Equipment – Leased

Capital Equipment – Leased			
Equipment	Quantity	Monthly Lease Cost	Total
Mobilization/Treatment Plinths	2	$75.00	$150.00
IFC/Ultrasound Machine	1	$83.00	$83.00
Other	0	$ -	$ -
TOTAL			$233.00

Table 14.9 Operating Expenses

	Operating Expenses						
Month	Supplies	Licences and Permits	Cleaning Services	Leased Equipment	Accounting	Lawyer	Total Monthly
Jan	$1,384.50	$336.00	$ -	$233.00	$ -	$ -	$1,953.50
Feb	$842.75	$ -	$ -	$233.00	$ -	$ -	$1,075.75
March	$ -	$ -	$ -	$233.00	$ -	$ -	$233.00
April	$ -	$ -	$ -	$233.00	$ -	$ -	$233.00
May	$ -	$ -	$ -	$233.00	$ -	$ -	$233.00
June	$842.75	$ -	$ -	$233.00	$ -	$ -	$1,075.75
July	$1,384.50	$ -	$ -	$233.00	$ -	$ -	$1,617.50
Aug	$ -	$ -	$ -	$233.00	$ -	$ -	$233.00
Sep	$ -	$ -	$ -	$233.00	$ -	$ -	$233.00
Oct	$42.75	$ -	$ -	$233.00	$ -	$ -	$1,075.75
Nov	$ -	$ -	$ -	$233.00	$ -	$ -	$233.00
Dec	$842.75	$ -	$ -	$233.00	$ -	$ -	$1,075.75
TOTAL	$6,140.00	$336.00	$ -	$2,796.00	$ -	$ -	$9,272.00

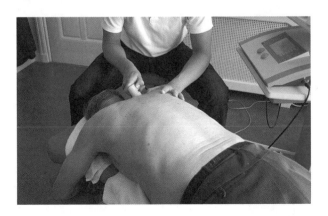

What is missing is the cost of utilities and upkeep if you are working out of your own space, any loans you will be paying interest on, wages paid to any employees (and yourself?), and marketing costs. So, let's keep going with "XX Clinic's" Year 1 projections …

Table 14.10 Utilities and Property Expenses

UTILITIES AND PROPERTY EXPENSES					
Month	Rent	Internet, Fax, Phone	Utilities	Insurance	Total Monthly
Jan	$ -	$450	$1,710	$145	**$2,305**
Feb	$ -	$130	$1,710	$145	**$1,985**
March	$ -	$130	$1,710	$145	**$1,985**
April	$1,944	$130	$655	$145	**$2,874**
May	$1,944	$130	$655	$145	**$2,874**
June	$1,944	$130	$800	$145	**$3,019**
July	$1,944	$130	$1,200	$145	**$3,419**
Aug	$1,944	$130	$1,200	$145	**$3,419**
Sep	$1,944	$130	$655	$145	**$2,874**
Oct	$1,944	$130	$655	$145	**$2,874**
Nov	$1,944	$130	$800	$145	**$3,019**
Dec	$1,944	$130	$1,500	$145	**$3,719**
TOTAL	**$17,496**	**$1,880**	**$13,250**	**$1,740**	**$34,366**

Notes and Assumptions:
1. Rent = 972 sq ft @ $24.00/sq ft (grossed up); 5-year lease
2. First three months of rent waived
3. Leaseholds paid by the building owner
4. Initial installation fees of $320.00 for Internet, fax, and phone services
5. Utilities include water ($0.4482/50 cubic meters), sewer ($0.4428/cubic meter + $25.02 service charge), electricity ($0.058/kWh)
6. Insurance includes liability ($1,200.00 for 2 million with no deductible), property ($120.00 for $120,000.00 with $2,500.00 deductible), and malpractice ($425.00 for 2 million with no deductible)

Table 14.11 Banking and Support Services

			Banking and Support Services							
Amount of Loan:			Term $20,000.00			Operating Line of Credit $50,000.00				
Month	Term Loan Principal Payments	Term Loan Interest Payments	Op Loan Balance	Op Loan Principal Payment	Op Loan Interest Payment	Accountant	Business Consultant	Bank Fees	Visa, MC, Interac	Total Monthly
Jan	$550.00	$1,250.00	$-	$-	$-	$800.00	$1,200.00	$25.00	$28.35	$3,853.35
Feb	$550.00	$1,171.88	$3,500.00	$-	$148.75	$-		$35.00	$28.35	$1,933.98
March	$550.00	$1,098.63	$15,500.00		$658.75	$-		$35.00	$28.35	$2,370.73
April	$550.00	$1,029.97	$25,500.00		$1,083.75	$500.00		$35.00	$28.35	$3,227.07
May	$550.00	$965.60	$30,500.00	$-	$1,296.25			$35.00	$116.78	$2,963.63
June	$550.00	$905.25	$31,500.00	$-	$1,338.75			$35.00	$62.19	$2,891.19
July	$550.00	$848.67	$36,500.00	$1,700.00	$1,551.25			$35.00	469.84	$4,754.76
Aug	$550.00	$795.63	$38,000.00	$1,700.00	$1,615.00			$40.00	$84.82	44,785.45
Sep	$550.00	$745.90	$42,500.00	$1,700.00	$1,806.25			$40.00	$80.21	$4,922.36
Oct	$550.00	$699.28	$42,500.00	$1,700.00	$1,806.25			$40.00	$78.95	$4,874.48
Nov	$550.00	$655.58	$42,500.00	$1,700.00	$1,806.25			$50.00	$141.31	$4,903.13
Dec	$550.00	$614.60	$40,694.00	$1,700.00	$1,729.50	$500.00		$50.00	$141.85	$5,285.94
TOTAL	$6,600.00	$10,780.97	$40,694.00	$10,200.00	$14,840.75	$1,800.00	$1,200.00	$455.00	$889.35	$46,766.07

1. Term loan @ prime plus 2 interest (est. 6.25%) with principal and interest payments expected to be complete in 36 months
2. Line of credit @ prime (est. 4.25%) – interest is only calculated on the principal drawn from the available credit limit (not expected to exceed $42,500.00)
3. Credit card and Interac fees are based on 60% of cash receipts in this form, and a 1.75% charge per transaction plus the monthly fee of $28.00
4. Banking fees are based on $25.00 per month loan charge, plus an initial $10.00 account service charge which increases over time to $25.00
5. A business consultant's services have been selected in lieu of legal, IT, and business services – this consultant is a barrister by profession

Table 14.12 Marketing

Marketing								
Month	Printing	Postage	Open House	Yellow Pages	Sponsor-ships	Web site	News-paper	Total Monthly
Jan	$700	$300	$480	$72	$ -	$2,500	$930	**$4,982**
Feb	$ -	$ -	$ -	$72	$ -	$250	$100	**$422**
March	$ -	$ -	$ -	$72	$ -	$250	$100	**$422**
April	$ -	$ -	$ -	$72	$1,500	$250	$100	**$1,922**
May	$ -	$ -	$ -	$72	$ -	$250	$100	**$422**
June	$500	$200	$ -	$72	$ -	$250	$100	**$1,122**
July	$ -	$ -	$ -	$72	$ -	$250	$100	**$422**
Aug	$ -	$ -	$ -	$72	$ -	$250	$100	**$422**
Sep	$ -	$ -	$ -	$72	$1,500	$250	$100	**$1,922**
Oct	$ -	$ -	$ -	$72	$ -	$250	$100	**$422**
Nov	$ -	$ -	$ -	$72	$ -	$250	$100	**$422**
Dec	$ -	$ -	$ -	$72	$ -	$250	$100	**$422**
TOTAL	**$1,200**	**$500**	**$480**	**$864**	**$3,000**	**$5,250**	**$100**	**$13,324**

Table 14.13 Cash Flow Statement

CASH FLOW STATEMENT

	Month 1	Month 2	Month 3	Month 4	Month 5	Month 6	Month 7	Month 8	Month 9	Month 10	Month 11	Month 12	Monthly Total
Cash Inflows													
Cash Receipts	$2,306	$6,918	$13,836	$23,060	$23,060	$23,060	$23,060	$23,060	$23,060	$23,060	$23,060	$23,060	$230,600
Term Loan	$20,000	$-	$-	$-	$-	$-	$-	$-	$-	$-	$-	$-	$20,000
Operating Loan	$-	$3,500	$12,000	$10,000	$5,000	$1,000	$5,000	$1,500	$4,500	$-	$-	$1,806	$40,694
Personal Investment	$-	$-	$-	$-	$-	$-	$-	$-	$-	$-	$-	$-	$-
Total Cash Inflows	$22,306	$10,418	$25,836	$33,060	$28,060	$28,060	$28,060	$24,560	$27,560	$23,060	$23,060	$21,254	$291,294
Cash Outflows													
Marketing	$4,982	$422	$422	$1,922	$422	$1,122	$422	$422	$1,922	$422	$422	$422	$13,324
Wages	$-	$-	$-	$-	$-	$-	$-	$-	$-	$-	$-	$-	$-
Bank Fees & Loan Payments	$3,853	$1,934	$2,371	$3,227	$2,875	$2,857	$4,713	$4,729	$4,870	$4,824	$4,790	$5,172	$46,215
Fixed Assets	$15,356	$-	$-	$-	$-	$-	$-	$-	$-	$-	$-	$-	$15,356
Operating Expenses	$1,954	$1,076	$233	$233	$233	$1,076	$1,618	$233	$233	$1,076	$233	$1,076	$9,272
Utilities & Property	$2,305	$1,985	$1,985	$2,874	$2,874	$3,019	$3,419	$3,419	$2,874	$2,874	$3,019	$3,719	$34,366
Total Cash Outflows	$28,450	$5,416	$5,011	$8,256	$6,404	$8,074	$10,171	$8,803	$9,899	$9,196	$8,464	$10,389	$118,533
Opening Cash Balance	$-	$6,144	$1,142	$19,683	$44,487	$66,143	$82,129	$100,018	$115,775	$133,435	$147,300	$161,896	
Increase/Decrease Cash	$6,144	$5,002	$20,825	$24,804	$21,656	$15,986	$17,889	$15,757	$17,661	$13,864	$14,596	$10,865	
Closing Cash Balance	$6,144	$1,142	$19,683	$44,487	$66,143	$82,129	$100,018	$115,775	$133,435	$147,300	$161,896	$172,761	

So, "XX Clinic" now has income of **$291,294** and expenditures of **$118,533** leaving a balance of **$172,761**. Again, this looks like a pretty nice earning potential. What you need to remember is that $60,000 of this came in the form of loans that must be repaid with interest. More importantly, the greatest cost of doing business is the cost of personnel.

At this point you have not paid yourself a wage or benefits. You have also not indicated that you will have the assistance of administrative help. In fact, many new business owners do count on a spouse or partner's income for living expenses and benefits in the start-up year, but this does not allow you to reflect the true cost of doing business and makes planning more difficult. It is, of course, not a sustainable position and will make investors uncomfortable. If you wish to keep costs down in Year 1 – when there are numerous major expenditures in other areas – a better approach might be to take a decreased salary and do your own administrative work such as answering client calls, booking clients, and doing the bookkeeping for the business. This is feasible but does take an organized individual and one who recognizes that the time spent doing the administration is time not spent with clients. In the long run, that means you are paying a hefty cost for that approach because, in health care, you cost more as the professional than paying a small business administrator such as a receptionist or secretary. You also lose revenue because you are not providing direct service. A reasonable goal is to be making a salary equivalent to your profession in competing sectors by the end of Year 3 of your business. In the end, one of the advantages of being in the private sector is to have the potential of earning more than you might otherwise. You will make some goals in your visioning for the business regarding when and how you plan to do so.

What about the loans? It is extremely unlikely that an investor, whether a bank, another lending institution, a family member, a friend, or a partner will agree to lending funds to you for your business if you have not put in your own money up front. Each institution will have its own guidelines on what percentage of the required funding they are ready to invest and it is usually directly related to the percentage you yourself are willing to commit.

Remember, theoretically, "everything's negotiable." But if the "XX Clinic" was a new venture, and the owner(s) did not have a track record of running a business successfully, they would be required to commit approximately $30,000 or more themselves when applying for a $60,000 loan. This commitment is used to demonstrate that the business owner is willing to shoulder a significant proportion of the financial risk for the endeavour.

Back to the money you made. If you are building a not-for-profit business, earnings over costs or profits are put back into the business to help sustain and improve it. In the end, and regardless of your personal financial goals, as the owner(s) of your business, you should plan to put some of the profits back into the business annually. You will need this initially for stability, subsequently for growth, and on an ongoing basis for ensuring that your business keeps up with equipment maintenance, clinical and technical advances, and remains competitive in the human resources market.

Now that you have gotten your feet wet trying to manipulate your financial projections using the spreadsheets to enter the numbers and the notes to detail where they came from, let's look at the overall picture of the financial status of the business. For this process, accountants use three primary forms of reporting, that is, three key financial statements: the **Balance Sheet**, the projected **Income Statement**, and the **Cash Flow** projections.

14.4 The Balance Sheet

Balance sheets are designed to show what the assets and liabilities, and thus the net worth of a company, are at a single point in time. Your company's assets include cash, inventory, accounts receivable, and fixed assets. Liabilities are essentially the monies you have to pay in less than 12 months, including wages, short-term loans (including credit card balances), taxes, and the final increments of long-term loans. A long-term liability may be a mortgage or long-term loan. The assets on a balance sheet will always equal the liabilities plus the owner's **equity**. The owner's equity is the total assets of the business minus the business' liabilities and is considered equal to the **net worth** of the business.

Let's use "XX Clinic" again to illustrate a **Balance Sheet** and to see what the net worth of the business is suggested to be at "start-up" and at the end of Year 1 (assuming there are no "accounts receivable," that is, money owed to the business by clients).

Table 14.14 Balance Sheet

Assets		
	Start-up	**Year 1**
Current Assets		
Cash	$20,000	$172,761
Accounts Receivable		$0
Inventory		
TOTAL Current Assets	**$20,000**	**$218,881**
Fixed Assets		
Cost of Fixed Assets		$9,005
Less: Accumulated Depreciation		$1,801
TOTAL Fixed Assets	$-	$7,204
TOTAL ASSETS	**$20,000**	**$226,085**
Liabilities & Owner's Equity		
Liabilities		
Accounts Payable		
Term Loans Payable	$20,000	$13,400
Operating Loans Payable	$-	$40,694
TOTAL Liabilities	**$20,000**	**$54,094**
Owner's Equity		
Paid-in Capital	$-	$-
Retained Earnings		$171,991
Total Owner's Equity	$-	$171,991
Liabilities & Owner's Equity	**$20,000**	**$226,085**

14.5 The Income Statement

The Income Statement enables you to calculate your company's pre-tax profits by subtracting total expenses from total revenues. It is also known as the **profit and loss statement**. The Balance Sheet then, gives you a static picture of the business at a single moment in time, for example, at year end. The Income Statement, on the other hand, provides a moving picture of the business during a particular period of time.

Taking a look at XX Clinic at the end of Year 1 again, the Income Statement predicts a very healthy net income: the income (profit) shown after all operating and non-operating income and expense, reserves, income taxes, minority interest, and extraordinary items, of $186,831. In fact, as outlined above, without taking out the cost of wages and benefits, and accounting for your administration time and its resultant loss of revenue-generating time, this is a very misleading number.

Table 14.15 Income Statement

Income Statement	
	Year 1
Revenue	
Gross Revenue	$276,720
Revenue	**$276,720**
Expenditures	
Marketing	$13,324
Wages & Benefits	$-
Non-Capital Assets	$6,351
Bank Fees	$3,794
Loan Interest Payments	$20,981
Operating Assumptions	$9,272
Utilities	$34,366
Depreciation	$1,801
Expenditures	**$89,889**
Net Income	**$186,831**

14.6 Cash Flow Projections

Cash flow projections are perhaps your most valuable tool for your financial planning. They provides an estimate of when and how much money will be received and paid out of a business over time. Cash Flow spreadsheets usually record cash flow on a month-by-month basis for a period of several years. *It has been suggested that using this tool well will be the difference between the success and failure of a small business.*

Cash flow projections help you to know where the cash comes from, when you need it, how much you will need, how much you will make, and how to time your expenditures in order to avoid cash shortages. This is where you can see very clearly when costs are greater than revenues, both in the short-term and for longer periods. If your planning has been good, your cash flow should be too.

How is "XX Clinic's" cash flow in Year 1? Flip back to Table 14.13 and see. There is a negative closing cash balance in the first two months of business, but then the company moves into the black, or positive position. Although this suggests the business becomes healthy very quickly, your banker and accountant will insist that you cannot be in a negative position and that you should use your operating loan (line of credit) to cover that loss. Over time, the income will exceed expenditures without using borrowed funds. This is when the business is truly in the black. In this case, the clinic owner would have actually committed thousands of his/her own dollars at the outset, adding to the income side of the picture. On the negative side, as before and not showing on our spreadsheet, is the wages component.

Let's go back to "XX Clinic" and revise the plan to include a salary for the owner as well as the addition of an individual hired to function as a combination receptionist/ aide/bookkeeper.

Table 14.16 Wages and Benefits

Owner – Clinician						
Month	Salary	EI	CPP	EHT	Benefits	Total Monthly
January	$4,000	$-	$-	$-	$-	$4,000
February	$4,000	$-	$-	$-	$-	$4,000
March	$4,000	$-	$-	$-	$-	$4,000
April	$4,000	$-	$-	$-	$-	$4,000
May	$4,000	$-	$-	$-	$-	$4,000
June	$4,000	$-	$-	$-	$-	$4,000
July	$4,000	$-	$-	$-	$-	$4,000
August	$4,000	$-	$-	$-	$-	$4,000
September	$4,000	$-	$-	$-	$-	$4,000
October	$4,000	$-	$-	$-	$-	$4,000
November	$4,000	$-	$-	$-	$-	$4,000
December	$4,000	$-	$-	$-	$-	$4,000
TOTAL	$48,000	$-	$-	$-	$-	$48,000

Receptionist/Aide/Bookkeeper						
Month	Salary	EI	CPP	EHT	Benefits	Total Monthly
January	$2,240	$44	$96	$22	$107	$2,509
February	$2,240	$44	$96	$22	$107	$2,509
March	$2,240	$44	$96	$22	$107	$2,509
April	$2,240	$44	$96	$22	$107	$2,509
May	$2,240	$44	$96	$22	$107	$2,509
June	$2,240	$44	$96	$22	$107	$2,509
July	$2,240	$44	$96	$22	$107	$2,509
August	$2,240	$44	$96	$22	$107	$2,509
September	$2,240	$44	$96	$22	$107	$2,509
October	$2,240	$44	$96	$22	$107	$2,509
November	$2,240	$44	$96	$22	$107	$2,509
December	$2,240	$44	$96	$22	$107	$2,509
TOTAL	$26,880	$484	$1,056	$264	$1,284	$29,968

Notes and Assumptions:
1. Employee's wages will be subject to a negotiable increase after one year of service
2. Canada Pension Plan (CPP) is calculated at 4.95% and is matched by the owner
3. Employment Insurance (EI) is deducted from the employee paycheque at a rate of 1.98% with the owner adding 1.4 times this amount
4. Workers' Compensation Board (WCB) payments are calculated at 1.0%
5. The receptionist's salary is set at $15.00 per hour in Year 1 and assumes a work week of approximately 38.5 hours
6. Vacation pay is calculated at 4.79%
7. Benefits are competitive with local public health care provider systems at just under 21% of salary
8. Owner and staff educational days and registration costs are not included in Year 1

Now how does this change the picture for "Clinic XX"? Take a look at the Cash Flow spreadsheet below (Table 14.17) and compare it to the previous Cash Flow spreadsheet above (Table 14.13).

Table 14.17 Revised Cash Flow Statement

Revised Cash Flow Statement

	Month 1	Month 2	Month 3	Month 4	Month 5	Month 6	Month 7	Month 8	Month 9	Month 10	Month 11	Month 12	Monthly Total
Cash Inflows													
Cash Receipts	$2,306	$6,918	$13,836	$23,060	$23,060	$23,060	$23,060	$23,060	$23,060	$23,060	$23,060	$23,060	$230,600
Term Loan	$20,000	$-	$-	$-	$-	$-	$-	$-	$-	$-	$-	$-	$20,000
Operating Loan	$-	$3,500	$12,000	$10,000	$5,000	$1,000	$5,000	$1,500	$4,500	$-	$-	$1,806	$40,694
Personal Investment	$30,000	$-	$-	$-	$-	$-	$-	$-	$-	$-	$-	$-	$30,000
Total Cash Inflows	$52,306	$10,418	$25,836	$33,060	$28,060	$24,060	$28,060	$24,560	$27,560	$23,060	$23,060	$21,254	$321,294
Cash Outflows													
Marketing	$4,982	$422	$422	$1,922	$422	$1,122	$422	$422	$1,922	$422	$422	$422	$13,324
Wages&Benefits	$6,509	$6,509	$6,509	$6,509	$6,509	$6,509	$6,509	$6,509	$6,509	$6,509	$6,509	$6,369	$77,968
Bank Fees & Loan Payments	$3,853	$1,934	$2,371	$3,227	$2,875	$2,857	$4,713	$4,729	$4,870	$4,824	$4,790	$5,172	$46,215
Fixed Assets	$15,356	$-	$-	$-	$-	$-	$-	$-	$-	$-	$-	$-	$15,356
Operating Expenses	$1,954	$1,076	$233	$233	$233	$1,076	$1,618	$233	$233	$1,076	$233	$1,076	$9,272
Utilities & Property	$2,305	$1,985	$1,985	$2,874	$2,874	$3,019	$3,419	$3,419	$2,874	$2,874	$3,019	$3,719	$34,366
Total Cash Outflows	$34,959	$11,925	$11,520	$14,765	$12,913	$14,583	$16,680	$15,312	$16,408	$15,705	$14,973	$16,758	$196,501
Opening Cash Balance	$-	$17,348	$15,840	$30,156	$48,451	$63,598	$73,075	$84,455	$93,703	$104,854	$112,210	$120,297	
Increase/Decrease Cash	$17,348	$1,507	$14,316	$18,295	$15,147	$9,477	$11,380	$9,248	$11,152	$7,355	$8,087	$4,496	
Closing Cash Balance	$17,348	$15,840	$30,156	$48,451	$63,598	$73,075	$84,455	$93,703	$104,854	$112,210	$120,297	$124,793	

The bottom line is now a closing balance of **$124,793** at year end. Of this amount, $90,694 is personal investment and loans. That leaves $34,099 of actual revenues over expenditures. This does not look as good as the previous projection of $112,761 ($172,761 - $60,000), but it is more realistic because you have paid yourself and have considered the cost of a receptionist in the mix, ensuring you have time to do the clinical work you need to do in order to keep revenues up. In addition, you do not have a single month where there is a predicted deficit (negative closing balance). Similarly, there is enough in your accounts as a contingency to cover any unknown crisis.

What we have looked at so far, are projections of what the business might look like financially, based on a wide range of carefully considered and researched assumptions, ranging from forecasts regarding the health care system and the economy, to detailed projections of service fees and business costs. Financial statements that depict a future period are called **pro-forma financial statements**. Current conventions in small business suggest that projections covering 3 years are sufficient. Fewer than that and you may miss some critical pieces of the picture, which may affect the viability of the business. For example, you may be optimistic about the **break-even point** for your business. Simply put, this is the point where your business is neither making a profit nor losing money. You, your partner(s), and/or your investors want to know when you achieve this critical state in the business as a measure of the viability of the business. This breakeven point can fluctuate in any given month early in the business, so you cannot stipulate you are at the breakeven point until the trend is stable. Similarly, if you try to predict your financial status for much longer than three years, it becomes more and more of a guessing game, and less and less precise. Once you have been in business for several years, then a five-year plan is not unreasonable; your past history helps to define your assumptions more accurately.

Once you have your first business plan in place and you open your doors, financial advisors suggest you sit down once a week to look at the bookkeeping, review how you are doing, and revise the plan and cash flow as required. The best advice we can give is to hire an accountant to set up your system and later perform financial audits; you may also hire someone to do your day-to-day bookkeeping, BUT make sure you understand and **review your books personally on a regular basis**. It is your responsibility in the end and it will be a great source of piece of mind.

RERERENCES

Edmonds, M., Schell, P. & Hopkins-Rosseel (2007). Financial statement templates. (CD-ROM enclosure). In D. Hopkins-Rosseel & B. Roulston. *Business in Clinical practice: How to get there from here*. Ottawa, ON: CAOT Publications ACE

CHAPTER 15
The Boundaries: Regulatory and Professional Issues
DIANA H. HOPKINS-ROSSEEL,DEC, BSC(PT), MSC(REHAB), MCPA

You have done so much planning at this point that it may feel like the end of the process. But there are a couple more tasks you are recommended to complete to ensure that you haven't put yourself in legal jeopardy. Just as it is not an acceptable defence to say you did not realize you could not drive through a red light, a practising clinician cannot claim ignorance of the laws and regulations governing clinical practice, or small business ownership and management. Therefore, take some time to investigate these boundaries and then document them in a small section at the end of your written business plan. This will help ensure that you have done "due diligence" with respect to seeking out the existing relevant legislation governing your business and clinical practices. It will also assist you in recognizing your limitations in interpreting and understanding those documents.

15.1 The Legislation and Regulatory Imperatives

A lawyer once suggested that there may be over 62 pieces of legislation in any given jurisdiction dictating how to, and how not to, legally open and run a clinical practice as a small business in Canada! That is a bit frightening, given that not many clinical professionals are also lawyers. This is the reason why we hire a lawyer to guide us during the planning and implementation of a business. Having said that, it is still important to record and understand the relevant contents of some key legislation directly related to your proposed business.

As you build your plan, document the acts and regulations that you will be responsible for following and communicating to your staff. Perhaps the best method is to separate this section into two primary components: 1) small business and 2) clinical practice. List and provide a short one-or-two-line synopsis of each one you consider important. This section can then be copied into the Policies and Procedures Manual for audit and staff training purposes.

15.1.1 Small Business

This is the section where you would note, for example: the *Employee Standards Act* and any related occupational health and safety legislation; business privacy legislation; laws dictating electronic equipment, billing, and documents use; insurance legislation; tax legislation; name registration by-laws; and landlord tenant legislation. If your business is located inside the confines, either physically and/or operationally, of another institution, you may also need to document any legislation that applies to this arrangement. For instance, using a pool in an adjacent space or sharing the services of a receptionist, might direct you to safety or contract legislation.

15.1.2 Health Care

As with the section above, list and briefly describe the contents of the legislation and regulations for all clinical practices and clinical employee groups. These might include: health care privacy and confidentiality legislation; consent legislation; health professions legislation, including competency and mandatory reporting regulations; and child services legislation. For all regulated health professionals in your jurisdiction, there is likely to be a comprehensive "omnibus" act encompassing all of the clinical professionals, within which will be smaller, individual professions' acts. For assistance with finding and understanding this material, you may contact the regulatory bodies of each clinical employee group you are responsible for and their practice advisors will get you started.

Once you have put this section together, make an appointment with the lawyer you have selected to be your legal consultant and have him/her review the information, and confirm that you have sufficient scope and understanding of the pieces you need to implement and oversee.

15.2 Professional Issues

Now, one last chance to size up what you are up against in the health care niche you are planning to conquer! Make a quick list of the one to three current and/or foreseeable issues with the significant potential to impact on your business. If the profession just changed its **educational** system from a Master of Science qualification to a Doctor of Science one, this is likely to impact on your hiring practices, salaries, external credibility, and inter-professional relationships. Write it down so that you are not blindsided by the change; instead, it gives you time to think about it and plan for your response(s).

Another good example would be to know and document that a competitor's employees are in the process of becoming unionized. This could mean you have upcoming competition in **human resources** (and you may need to increase salaries and benefits) or you may face possible labour shortage issues.

Following and interpreting the rapidly progressive trends in **information technology** (IT) is a must for any clinical private practice these days. New practice management software, wireless systems, and/or e-billing options can dramatically improve the efficiency and income of your practice. Day-to-day activities, financial transactions and accounting, annual program evaluations and quality assurance, as well as all business and clinical communications may all be improved; issues such as client confidentiality, however, may weigh against these advantages. Knowing the position that governments, regulatory bodies, and professional associations are taking on each new IT advancement will let you realize the advantages of adopting IT systems without putting your business at risk.

On a wider scale you could note pending changes in **legislation** affecting one of your client groups. For example, if the government is planning to legislate the public funding of geriatric community services and you are implementing a home care private practice, you may be able to procure the government contract for your area.

There may also be evolving **regulatory** issues to keep an eye on. For instance, the potential to have a specialist designation process introduced in one regulated health profession but not another with a competing scope of practice, has the potential to give the former group a significant marketing advantage over the latter.

Even the advancing emphasis on the **ethical dimensions** of clinical practice in the business sector can have a dramatic impact on the parameters of the health and growth of your business. These might include professional boundaries with respect to interpersonal interactions, conflict of interest situations, or personal morals conflicting with, for example, professional codes of ethics. What if ethically it would be in the best interests of certain clients to be treated but the costs to you are prohibitive? For example, the profession's Standards of Practice stipulate that a client who has a communicable disease should not be turned away. But what if their attendance at your clinic would require increased staff time and effort to provide an isolated space for treatment, and disinfecting of equipment and surfaces following treatment?

If you don't follow the issues in the foreground of your profession and those in the federal and provincial/territorial sectors, you risk losing both key market sectors and opportunities. Similarly, you risk being sanctioned for, or losing business because of, uninformed business decisions. Make a conscious effort to track these changes regularly via professional association and regulatory body communications and the news media, and you will see clear benefits to your clinical practice.

CHAPTER 16
Tying it all Up:
Confidentiality and Recognition of Risks
DIANA H. HOPKINS-ROSSEEL,DEC, BSC(PT), MSC(REHAB), MCPA

se that the right to trial by jury is a constitutional
rty, after consulting with counsel of their choice
mutual benefit waives any right to trial by jury i
rmance or enforcement of this Contract.

ed has signed this Contract

SIGNATURE

This is it … you can see the light at the end of the tunnel! One final piece to fit into the puzzle: managing your risks. You need to convince yourself, any partners or associates, and your investor(s) that you understand there are risks involved in the venture, you know what those risks are and, most importantly, you have put contingencies in place to mitigate those risks. If you suggest, overtly or by omission, that there are no significant risks, a savvy potential associate or investor will run the other way, not wanting to become involved with someone who is either that naïve or that obtuse. This can translate into your having a tough time finding financing for the venture.

16.1 Mitigating the Risks

Negative, unexpected, and even unlikely events will have the greatest impact. They need to be acknowledged and safeguards put in place against them.

16.1.1 A Few Examples

1. Your business is a community service, requiring a car for each employee to travel between clients. The risk is mechanical failure. The plans to mitigate the risk may be to: lease the vehicles; have a surplus vehicle ready to use while an other is under repair; have a regular maintenance schedule; have a line of credit sufficient to allow for occasional car rental.

2. You will be purchasing the building your clinic will be housed in. The risk is substantial, and there could be unexpected electrical, plumbing, or structural failures. The plans to minimize the impact on your revenue generation are to: purchase sufficient insurance coverage to cover the repair costs; hire a contract maintenance worker or service; ensure you arrange for a detailed building inspection prior to purchasing the site; have an operational loan with sufficient funds to cover salaries and overheads for any short shutdown period.

3. Your revenues depend on full staffing. The risk is that an employee becomes ill or resigns. Your plan is to ensure that: all staff descriptions and hiring policies regarding qualifications allow you to train each employee to provide any services that the other employees provide that are within their legal scope of practice, so as to cover short term illnesses or absences; budget projections assume an average of 21 or fewer working days a month and up to 11 paid sick days a year per employee; salaries and benefits that are sufficiently competitive to optimize staff retention.

The idea is to run through a day, a week, a month in the life of the business; think of every possible scenario costing delays, outlay of funds, and/or revenue losses. Then put in place any financially and logistically possible protections you can prior to opening the business. Prove to yourself and your colleagues that your contingency plans make the venture well worth the inherent risks.

TAKE HOME MESSAGE
Hope for the best.
Corollary:
Plan for the worst.

16.2 Statement of Confidentiality

Last but not least, make sure you include a statement of confidentiality in your business plan. This is not a statement of client or personal information confidentiality; rather, it is a statement that ensures your entire business plan is protected from other individuals plagiarizing or using it for their own purposes. You do not want to do all this research and planning only to find out that someone else is profiting from your hard work.

16.2.1 Example of a Statement of Confidentiality
"This business plan is strictly confidential and may not be communicated or reproduced, in full or in part, without the expressed written consent of all of the owners and associates, (place full names here).

Have your lawyer review the statement and revise it as they see fit to give you and your partner(s) maximum protection against theft of your original ideas and the results of your efforts.

That, as they say, is that.
You are done. You have a business plan.
Congratulations!

Remember, many new ventures will go through numerous incarnations, but the moments of satisfaction will come to outnumber the moments of pure terror.
Enjoy.

CHAPTER 17
Running the Show: Keeping Your Business Afloat
ALICE B. AIKEN, PT, Ph.D

So, you have your business plan together and you have started your business, that's great! What do you think is the most important thing when it comes to keeping that business going? Cash flow of course! You will find that cash flows out pretty easily, but having it come in can be a challenge. It is also a challenge to not only keep your referral base up, but also get the cash in hand. However, there are a few simple steps you can take to ensure that your cash flow continues to be a flow and not a trickle. Knowing the options and choosing what works best for you is the key. We will explore this topic under the following headings: 1) billing; 2) insurance company interface; and 3) business communications.

17.1 Billing

This is your primary source of revenue generation, so knowing how to do it well will ensure that you manage your business successfully.

Warren has had a private physical therapy clinic in a downtown venue for two years. On paper, his monthly billings should be covering all his expenses, yet he is constantly dipping into his business line of credit to pay bills and employees at the end of the month. He can't figure out what is going wrong. He has three full-time *physical therapists, including himself, generating income; he employs one full-time office worker, and one part-time physical therapy assistant. He has the regular monthly bills (rent, utilities, communications, and equipment loans) and he feels that his business plan should be working. One day he asks Wendy, his office worker, to generate a report on outstanding billing and he finds that he has $85,000 in accounts receivable, $50,000 of them older than 120 days! Warren is shocked. How could this have happened?*

There are many strategies for effective billing and you can use one or all of them. You must ensure that the money is coming in and that it is coming in promptly. It is not unusual to have outstanding billings for 30 or even 45 days; that is sometimes how long it takes for cheques to come in from insurance companies. Anything over 60 days, however, will be harder for you to track and collect.

17.1.1 Methods for the Effective Collection of Bills: Pros, Cons, and Solutions

Pay-as-you-go entails billing all clients on the day of their appointment. Ensure that you accept all methods of payment: credit cards, debit, cheques, and cash so everyone has a means by which they can pay. Issue receipts immediately so your clients may claim from their insurance company in a timely fashion.

PROS

1. The business is never out of pocket for cash; whatever you have billed, you will have on hand and you can run your business smoothly.

2. You can avoid those who will take services and not pay for them, or object after the fact to what they were charged.

CONS

1. Canadians are not used to paying for health care and this may rub some people the wrong way. It may cost you clients.

2. Not everyone can afford to pay for every visit when they are there. It may be close to a payday, or they may not be able to afford to come so they will miss their appointment rather than admit that they are unable to pay.

3. People may be lazy about sending in their receipts to get paid by their insurance company, and at some point they may decide they are out of pocket too much money and stop coming.

4. This is a lot of work for your front desk staff; they already have numerous other tasks to do and this can be very time consuming.

SOLUTIONS

1. Bill every second or third visit, but ensure that you keep a photocopy of the client's credit card on file in case they don't return. This will ensure you always have a manner in which to obtain your money. If they do not wish to do this, then explain that you will have to bill every visit separately.

2. Ensure that you tell all clients about the policy when they book their first appointment; this will avoid unnecessary surprises and unpleasant confrontations.

3. If you can afford it, train another staff member to be able to take calls and book appointments while your front desk person is busy with billing.

John has been a long-time client of the clinic and has always paid at every visit. One day, after his appointment, he tells you that he has had some unforeseen expenses and will not be able to pay today's session, but he will pay next time he is in. You tell him that is no problem, you will keep a copy of his credit card on file and bill every two or three visits, with his permission.

LESSON

Everyone can have financial issues. Try to accommodate your clients and still ensure that you are getting paid in a timely fashion. Never tell your clients they can't come just because they can't pay that day; always have an alternative solution.

Bill insurance companies and other third-party payers directly when you are able to do so, and bill everyone else on a "pay-as-you-go" basis.

PROS

1. Clients are not out of pocket when they come to visit, so they are more likely to be content coming for repeated visits if these are necessary.

2. You are guaranteed that the cheque you receive will be good, and you will get all your money.

CONS

1. The payment is not in hand directly, and may take up to six weeks to get back to you after you have billed the insurance company; if your cash flow is limited, you have to plan for this.

2. You have to know what portion of the bill each company covers for each specified group of workers so that you can charge any co-payments to the clients.

3. If you do not charge the appropriate co-payment you may not get that portion of the money from the client, or you may end up owing that person some money back.

4. You have to check with each insurance company individually to see if they will allow you to third-party bill; they may not, and you may end up having to bill the client directly anyway.

SOLUTIONS

1. Keeping track of which insurance companies cover what proportion of the expenses can be an arduous task, but an organized office person can get that in hand very easily and keep track of it for you.

2. Ensure that you have the appropriate papers for your clients' signatures for each insurance company so you can make the billing process easy.

3. Bill at a set time, for example every third visit, so that you are sure the billing gets done and a constant flow of cash is being maintained. Also ensure someone is billed when they are discharged from care.

4. Go through your clients' financial files at regular intervals (for example once a month), to ensure that all billing is up-to-date.

You have two clients, Susan Smith and Ed Greene who are both schoolteachers with the same school board. They are both insured through the Greatest Insurance Company in the West. Susan is a high school teacher, Ed is an elementary school teacher, and you have the foresight to call the insurance company to check if they have the same coverage. To your surprise, you discover that Susan has 100% coverage, Ed only has 80% coverage and must make a co-payment. You have just saved yourself a lot of back-tracking and billing problems.

LESSON

Insurance companies insure many different groups of workers, even ones who may seem similar. The health care coverage that each group of workers has is negotiated by their union or staff association and may be very different from another group insured by the same company. So, the same company, and even the same type of worker, may have very different types of coverage. Always check when a client comes to your clinic for the first time.

Bill only guaranteed third-party payers, such as your local workers' compensation unit or pre-approved frameworks through automobile insurance companies, and bill the rest of your clients with the pay-as-you-go method.

PROS

1. These organizations will send you the paperwork to bill them with the client, and they will pay, provided you treat within their guidelines.

2. You will receive all your money, usually in a timely manner, and your billing will be up-to-date.

CONS

1. Generally these organizations do not pay the full fees of the clinic, so you may have to bill less for these "guaranteed payment" organizations.

2. These organizations typically require numerous forms to be filled out to ensure that your services are warranted; this can be a very time-consuming task.

3. You may have services cut-off retroactively, so you may not get all your payment from the company, and you may have to approach the client for payment.

SOLUTIONS

1. Ensure that you are aware of how many visits a client is allowed when you start treating them.

2. Ensure that you are aware of any pre-approved frameworks that must be followed when treating these clients.

3. Become familiar with the forms that must be filled out, and keep up the communication with the payer to ensure that you do not lose money.

Your client Kate has been off her job as a daycare worker for six months due to a shoulder injury. She is almost fully better, and has returned to work part-time with modified duties. She is being covered by workers' compensation, but they want to cut off her benefits and send her back to work full-time right away. You fill out an extension form and outline the treatment timeline for Kate to return to full duties and finish physical therapy. Compensation agrees to continue paying for Kate's physical therapy for the next four weeks.

LESSON

> Regular updates showing client progression, will allow you to work with guaranteed third-party payers to ensure that you receive your money, and that the client is being treated in a manner designed to rehabilitate them.

17.2 Insurance Company Interface

Interaction with insurance companies is a necessary part of clinical life, even if you are billing your clients directly. These companies are still paying for your services and from time to time, they may require communication from you.

Catherine has had a successful private practice as an audiologist for 10 years. She regularly bills insurance companies for appliances that she prescribes and sells to her customers. Catherine always ensures that she sends the physician referral and her report to the company to ensure that she gets billed. Suddenly she notices that one of the companies she is used to billing has not paid her in over eight weeks. Catherine calls the company to find out why, and they say that their policies have changed, they will only issue cheques to their clients, and they will no longer third-party bill. Catherine asks why they didn't inform her of this change, and they tell her that it is her job to keep up with changes that they make.

Unfortunately, the insurance company is correct. Changes take place to existing policies all the time and this can seriously affect your billing of these companies. Groups of workers can switch insurers without knowing that this has taken place, and if you send a bill to the incorrect company, they are not bound to inform you of the error; you will only find out when the payment doesn't arrive. In addition, you will sometimes get two different stories from two different workers at the same insurance company. Always ask for any policies to be faxed or e-mailed to you, so you have the information in writing and can relay it back to the workers if they dispute what you were told.

So how do you stay informed on both insurance companies and how different groups of workers are insured?

17.2.1 Strategies to Interface with Insurance Companies

1. If you have not seen your client for a while, ask them if they are aware of any changes to their existing insurance policy.

2. If you see a particular group of workers on a regular basis, call the insurance company at regular intervals to ensure that your billing meets their standards and that they have not changed any aspect of the policy.

3. If changes have been made to a policy for a particular group of workers, ask for these changes to be faxed or e-mailed to you so you can keep track of them.

4. Inform your clients if you find out about changes to their policy so they are aware of this for any other health professionals they may visit.

5. If you get two different versions of a regulation within a policy from two different workers, do not be afraid to contact the manager of the section; they would rather know that their employees are unclear on a policy then have complaints sent to them from their clients.

6. Be fair and judicious in your billing. Do not over-bill or charge irregular fees if an insurance company will pay more for a service than you usually charge. This is not a fair or sound business practice, and if the insurance company finds out, they may cut you off as a provider of services for their clients.

17.3 Business Communications

Effective communication is an essential tool to the success of every business. Not only must you communicate effectively and efficiently with your clients and your third-party payers, you must also communicate effectively with your suppliers, contractors, financial personnel, and anyone else who can have an impact on your business.

Lisa is an occupational therapist with a business that involves prescribing assistive devices and appliances for clients with any type of mobility problem. She is contacted by the director of a nursing home who wishes to have a client with Parkinson's assessed for eating difficulties. The director asks Lisa to come at six o'clock the next day to watch the client feed. Lisa agrees and shows up at 6:00 pm to observe the client having supper. To her dismay, the client is in bed reading, and the nursing staff informs her that the client had his dinner at 5:00 pm. Lisa contacts the director the next morning, and the director is quite upset and tells Lisa she expected her at 6:00 am to watch the client have breakfast. She does not end up hiring Lisa for the job.

Lisa is the professional, and as such has the responsibility of ensuring that her business survives. It is essential that she is clear in all her dealings with anyone who wants to hire her, or whom she wishes to hire.

The main components of business communications to consider are:
1. Business Ethics
2. Business Writing Skills
3. Communication in the Workplace
4. Conflict Resolution
5. Creative Thinking
6. Consumer Relations

17.3.1 Business Ethics

Always deal with clients and other companies as you wish to be dealt with. Using sound business ethics will ensure that even if you find yourself in a difficult situation, you have the comfort of knowing it was an honest mistake. Businesses that use unsound ethical practices rarely survive. In addition, word will get around that you are not a business to be dealt with on any level.

You are asked by your friend Ed, the lawyer, to assess a client who was in a motor vehicle accident. The client's name is Susan. Susan feels she has not been treated fairly by her insurance company and now has a personal injury lawsuit against them. You assess Susan and can find no reason why she has not returned to work, her functioning is full and pain free. Ed asks you not to write a report or share this information with the insurance company. In the meantime, Susan has given your name to the insurance company and they contact you to ask for a copy of the report.

This is a difficult case. You will have to receive permission from Susan to share the information with her insurance company; but if she has given your name to the insurance company and the case goes to court, your name could come up. This is a tricky situation, but if Ed is a true friend he will understand that you have to practice ethically and write the report, or it will be more than one lawsuit that is lost. It will be your professional reputation as being an ethical business person.

17.3.2 Business Writing Skills
Effective business writing involves knowing why you are writing a letter, understanding the needs of the reader, and then clearly and concisely writing what you need to say. It is easy to follow the seven "Cs" of business letter writing. You should be:
- clear
- concise
- correct
- courteous
- conversational
- convincing
- complete

When you write a letter, you are trying to convince the recipient to act or react in a positive way. The recipient will respond appropriately if your meaning is very clear. Try to always write a sincere and helpful letter; this will help to identify the tone of your small business.

17.3.3 Communication in the Workplace
In order to really understand business communication, it is essential to know that miscommunication is normal. When speaking with others, we frame our thoughts using our view of the world. This transmission, when perceived by someone else, is framed using their view of the world, so their interpretation of what we say is not identical to what they hear. In general speech, this is not a problem, but in the workplace, miscommunication can be a costly error.

Dana runs a successful private physiotherapy practice. She relies heavily on her office manager Denise when it comes to billing and accounts receivable. One day Dana asks Denise to do all the past billing for 60 days. Denise is overwhelmed by the work, and when Dana takes a break from seeing clients, she finds a distraught Denise trying to catch up on all the billing for the last two months. Dana stops her and confirms that she just meant for her to do the accounts that were 60 days overdue, not everything for the last two months.

A simple error in communication; but had it not been corrected, it would have cost a lot of time and aggravation for the office manager. So, if we start with the idea that miscommunication is normal, we stand a much better chance of making communication work. Usually, people assume they are being clear, and that the problem lies with the other person. How many times a day have you said: "but, I thought you meant ...," or "I assumed you were talking about ...," or "you've completely misinterpreted what I was saying!" Miscommunications have become common and we don't think of the wider implications. It requires really hard work to make ourselves clear and ensure that we are understood by others.

Ensure that you communicate as effectively as possible in critical situations such as with colleagues and clients, in meetings, during disagreements, and at negotiations. Always ensure that the person with whom you are communicating understands what was said. Ask them to repeat it in their own words, and clarify any questions they may have. Communication in business is not something that should be left to chance.

17.3.4 Conflict Resolution

Conflict resolution can take many forms depending on the size of a company and the nature of the circumstances surrounding the conflict. In general, rehabilitation practices are small and issues of conflict can be dealt with in-house. It is essential that as an owner or manager, you are familiar with situations that can cause conflict, and deal with them in a timely and effective manner.

Jenny is a kinesiologist who owns a multidisciplinary home care rehabilitation facility. In addition to therapists, she has a secretary, Barb, and an assistant, Mary. Both are valued employees, integral to the smooth running of Jenny's business. Barb and Mary each believe they have seniority over the other, and they are starting to get the therapists involved in their conflict. Jenny notices the other employees starting to complain about how Barb and Mary treat each other. Jenny intervenes and has a meeting with both Barb and Mary. She outlines each of their jobs, tells them they are both key players in the success of the facility, and asks them to discuss any issues they may have in the secure environment of a meeting with the three of them. Barb and Mary are secure in their new duties; they feel they have cleared the air, and they start to work in a more collegial fashion.

It is important to understand some common causes of conflict and essential concepts of conflict resolution (Isenhart & Spangle, 2000):

▶ conflict spirals – if left unresolved, a minor conflict can escalate into a major dispute, one potentially irreversible in the minds of the people who are at odds;

▶ conflict styles – some people will want to talk about an issue of conflict, others will not; some will want to drag other employees into it, or try to get the attention of the manager so they can state their case;

▶ collaboration – working together as a cohesive unit for a common purpose;

▶ face saving – when a person has been found to be at fault for an incident, they may have a difficult time admitting it in front of you or the injured party; it is important to provide a comfortable method by which an individual can do this;

▶ intergroup conflicts – groups of workers may start to take sides in a conflict situation if management does not intervene at an early stage, creating a very uncomfortable and tension-filled work environment.

It is also essential to understand how open negotiation, with all parties present, is the key to resolving conflict. As a clinic owner or manager you will be called upon to be the facilitator of collaborative methods for resolving a dispute. It is imperative to be impartial, empathetic, confidential, and honest when dealing with any conflict situation.

17.3.5 Creative Thinking

In formal education, we are taught to think in a critical manner, to create a logical argument, figure out an answer, eliminate incorrect methodologies, and focus on the correct one. However, in order for a business to be successful, the owners and/or managers must also think in a critical manner, one that focuses on exploring ideas, generating possibilities, and looking for numerous right answers. Both types of thinking are essential to a successful business (Harris, 1998).

Table 17.1 Critical versus Creative Thinking

▼Critical Thinking	▼Creative Thinking
analytical	generating information
convergent	divergent
vertical	lateral
probability	possibility
judging	no judgement
focused	diffuse
objective	subjective
one answer	many answers
left brain	right brain
reasoning	richness
Yes but	Yes and

In any type of problem solving, both kinds of thinking are important. First, we must analyse a problem. Second, we should generate possible solutions. Third, we must choose and implement the best solution. Finally, we must evaluate the effectiveness of the solution and be willing to change it if necessary.

Randy has been operating a successful private physical therapy clinic for the past two years. His business has grown well, but he would like to market it to a wider group of people to attract clients. He thinks he should spend his money on an ad in the local newspaper; colleagues who own other clinics have told him this works well. He holds a staff meeting and shares his idea with his staff (an other therapist, a clinic secretary, and a part-time physical therapy assistant). They start discussing it and come up with several ideas that hadn't occurred to Randy. In the end he spends the same amount of money on sponsoring a local triathlon, handing out flyers in four new subdivisions in his city, and sending customized prescription pads to all the family physicians in town: a great use of creative thinking to solve a critical problem.

17.3.6 Consumer Relations

The customer is always right. This is a mantra, and in a small business it is essential that all employees believe this. However, this does not mean that clients can railroad you into doing things you should not do. But it does mean you must always treat them with courtesy and respect. If you treat even one client poorly, they will tell numerous people about it, and your business will start to get a bad reputation. If you treat all your customers well, they may not be as likely to talk about it, but they will refer friends and family to you because they had a pleasant experience at your business.

Gail is a secretary at a private speech language pathology clinic. Steve has been a client there for two months. Steve has just found out that his insurance will not cover the full cost of the visits. He is angry, and he starts getting loud when discussing the matter with Gail. He says she told him his insurance would cover the full amount, and he is not going to pay the co-payment that the company insists he should pay. Gail insists she did not know what his insurance would cover until she got the first bill back, and she says she told him that. Jennifer, the speech pathologist who owns the practice, quickly intervenes. She takes Steve aside and assures him that it was an honest error in communication, and that he must pay his bill, but they can work out a payment schedule that is convenient for him. She apologizes if Steve was surprised by the revelation, but she assures him it will not happen again. She has just ensured that Steve will leave satisfied, even if he does not return as a client.

If you are running a small business, a few simple steps can help you ensure that you keep the cash flowing in and your business afloat. Select a system for your billing that is organized and manageable for your business. Ensure that you keep in close contact with insurance companies so you understand their policies and get written material from them as often as possible. Finally, ensure that all your business communications are clear, succinct, honest, and inclusive. This will help you to run and build your business into what you desire it to be.

REFERENCES

Harris, R. (1998). *Introduction to Creative Thinking.* Retrieved April 29, 2007, from www.virtualsalt.com.

Isenhart, M.W., & Spangle, M. (2000). *Collaborative Approaches to Resolving Conflict.* Thousand Oaks, CA: Sage Publications.

PART II

P E R S O N A L F I N A N C E

BRADLEY ROUSLTON

CHAPTER 18

The Financial Hike and Packing Your Knapsacks

BRADLEY ROULSTON, BA, CFP, CLU, RHU

Remember the analogy we used in Chapter 4, that of your business plan being a roadmap? In Part II, you can now use that map and pack for your financial hike. All you need are a few essentials to put in your knapsack.

18.1 The Truth (It's Not so Bad)

The topic of financial planning is one of the world's great conversation stoppers. It joins the ranks of Star Trek conventions, stamp collections, and living in your parents' basement. Most people would rather close their eyes, hold their breath, and stick their fingers in their ears than talk about stocks, bonds, insurance, wills, or retirement funds.

The truth is that managing your finances isn't as frightening or as complicated as you might think. All it takes is a tight cap on your cash flow water bottle, an umbrella, a first-aid kit, a daypack, and a big retirement backpack. Imagine you're planning to go on a long hike - a financial hike. Over the course of this hike, you hope that your income will increase and you'll have the ability to pay not only for food and rent, but also emergencies, gifts, trips, and your retirement.

First, figure out where you want to hike to: these are your "Viewpoints." Once you find out where you are going, you can determine how to pack your cash flow water bottle, which consists of income faucets and expense, and debt and tax drains.

18.1.1 Put a Plug in It

You start on your hike, your income faucets are going fine, work is plentiful and there are lots of companies willing to loan you money - you feel that you deserve to buy a few things for yourself. You make a stop to drink in your riches and purchase one of your dream items. Then another and another.

Your luxurious cash supply is slowly disappearing because you forgot to put the cap back on your water bottle - or, in other words, use self-restraint. Controlling your spending through proper budgeting is one of your best weapons against the lure of yet another pair of shoes and eating out for the fourth week in a row. Using your money wisely means you'll be able to afford big-ticket items, such as a house or a cottage, sooner. Otherwise, you'll just be left thirsty. Wealth is created by how much you save, not necessarily by how much you make! As well, if you consume less, you can work less!

18.1.2 Good Debt and Bad Debt

During your dream knapsack spending spree, you incurred some debt. You maxed out your credit cards and bought a house. How do you know which debt to pay off first? The answer is simple: the bad debt (for more on debt management, see chapter 20).

18.1.3 Shelter from the Tax Storm

Your hike might start out sunny, but it eventually rains (it always does). Tax rain begins to eat away at your knapsacks and their valuable contents if you aren't prepared. The ground gets slippery, you're soaked, and suddenly you wish you were safe in your parents' basement!

REST STOP *Keeping your cash flow water bottle full of savings:*

▶ **Go on a spending diet and tighten your personal expense drain.**

▶ **Pay off bad debt first - don't let your credit card bills slide. Then focus on debt management strategies like paying your mortgage and choosing lower interest rates.**

▶ **Use your tax shelter umbrella to keep more of your money.**

Luckily, you have an umbrella. You open it and are miraculously sheltered from the tax storm. You've lost some of your cash, but not as much as you would have without your umbrella. It might be tempting to ditch your umbrella (after all, it's one more thing you have to carry), but resist. The extra effort is always worth it. Tax planning is an essential part of your financial hike (for more information on taxes, check out chapter 21).

18.2 Your Knapsacks

After your cash flow water bottle is planned for, you start to pack your knapsacks. You buy a first-aid kit, a daypack and a retirement backpack, and place them in a row in front of you.

The first one is for emergencies - it's your first-aid kit. In it you pack insurances, a will, some credit, and emergency cash. The second bag is your daypack. You toss in savings for your wildest fantasies. When it's full, this knapsack is bigger than your first-aid kit, but not as big as your third knapsack - the retirement backpack, which has to have enough rations in it to last for all of your retirement years. You carry these packs with you on your financial journey; their contents are your lifeline to a worry-free trip. (To get the complete picture on your three knapsacks, see chapter 22.)

18.2.1 That Wasn't so Bad

Now you know the basic elements of your financial hike: make sure you're armed with emergency cash and plans; save money for your dreams and spend it wisely; save a bundle for your retirement; seek shelter from taxes; and pay off bad debt first. Over the next few chapters, you'll learn more secrets for putting together a complete financial plan and how to apply these tricks to your personal life.

REST STOP *Your three packs:*

▸ Your first-aid kit is for emergency funds. Keep this bag light, but make sure you pack it well.

▸ Your daypack contains funds for trips, a wedding, a house, or starting your own business (or anything your heart desires). This bag empties and refills many times over the course of your hike.

▸ Your retirement backpack will support you when you stop working. Fill it to the brim! It needs to be bigger than most people think.

CHAPTER 19

Goal Setting

BRADLEY ROULSTON, BA, CFP, CLU, RHU

19.1 Where Do You Want to Go?

Everyone's going somewhere. You can choose to let life lead you where it wants, or you can take control and decide your own destinations. The key to getting where and what you want is goal setting. Take, for example, your job. You wouldn't be able to treat patients properly without goals. You'd have no idea if they were making appropriate progress or whether your treatment plan was a success. Financial planning is no different. Goal setting should be your first step to healthy finances.

On a Financial Hike, goal setting is determining which Viewpoints (Life goals) you want to achieve in your life. Your financial plan (or guidebook) will then outline what the best trail routes are and how to pack for your trips. Writing down your viewpoints is the most important step in your Financial Hike. How can you figure out what trails to take, how much cash flow you will need in your water bottle, or what to pack if you don't know where you're going? Examples of your viewpoints might be a wedding, buying a home, cottage or cabin, opening a clinic, getting out of debt, having children and helping them with their education, spending more time with your family, travelling, exercising more regularly, or retiring early yet comfortably. Buying a house will involve figuring how much money you will need to save for a down payment and what size mortgage your cash flow can handle. Spending more time with your family will require working less, impacting your income faucets. Either way, a financial guidebook will help.

19.2 Making it Happen

Take 10 minutes and write down all the things you want to happen in your life. Be as creative as you can, but make sure they are realistic. Then write a tentative time frame beside each wish.

Wishes	**Time**

Congratulations! You have just done what 90% of Canadians don't do: set goals and write them down. It's also important that you talk to people about your goals because then you're more likely to follow through with them. If you have a family, you need to set both individual and common goals. Just remember that your wishes are non-competitive - don't try to live up to someone else's expectations or match others' goals.

Most importantly, review your goals on a monthly basis. As your life changes, so might your dreams. Staying on top of your goals means that your financial plan will be proactive and change with you. Remember: money can't buy you happiness, but it can give you both security and freedom. Money finances your backpacks, which in turn blaze the trails to your life's viewpoints.

19.3 Current Assessment

Before you start planning for the future, you need to have a clear picture of where you stand today. Begin by looking at your:
- ▶ **assets and debts (what you own and what you owe);**
- ▶ **income and expenses (your cash flow).**

On a piece of paper, write down everything that you own and owe. The value of what you own is what someone else is willing to pay for it – so be realistic and leave your ego out. This is your **Balance Sheet**.

▼ Assets		▼ Liabilities	
Condo	$180,000	Mortgage	$165,000
Car	$8,000	Line of Credit	$2,000
Computer	$1,000	Owe Parents	$800
Bank Account	$2,500	Student Loans	$20,000
RSP	$8,000		
Investments	$2,000		
Sports Equipment	$800		
Total Assets	$202,300	Total Liabilities	$187,800
NET WORTH		**$14,500**	

On another piece of paper, write down all sources of annual income coming in (work, rental income, investment income, trust income, etc). Then write where all of your money is going (personal expenses, debt interest, and taxes). This is your Income Statement.

▼ Income	▼ Expenses
Employment Income	General (groceries, household, clothing, child care)
Pension	Housing (mortgage/rent, property taxes, insurance, maintenance, utilities, communications)
Family Allowance	Transportation (lease/finance payments, transit, insurance, gas, maintenance, parking)
Other Government Benefits Rental Income	Health Care (health insurance, life insurance, disability insurance, vision/dental, medication)
Investment Income	Recreaion (vacations, entertainment, dining, sports, hobbies, club membership, subscriptions)
Other	Miscellaneous (gifts, charity, other) Financial (registered and non-registered contributions, loan payments, credit card payments)
TOTAL INCOME	**TOTAL EXPENSES**

Adapted from Mackenzie Investements. (2007.) Can You Afford to Live in 2017? Burn Rate Workbook [Brochure]. Toronto, ON: Author.

It's also important to identify upcoming opportunities and challenges, such as jobs, marriage, divorce, children, and relocation expenses. This context will give you a baseline from which to create a feasible financial plan.

CHAPTER 20
Budgeting and Debt Management
BRADLEY ROULSTON, BA, CFP, CLU, RHU

20.1 Budgeting – Cash Flow Water Bottle Drains

Budgeting is an important part of managing your current and future finances. It can help you to track how much money is draining out of your water bottle of savings and how hard your income faucets need to run to keep it nicely topped up. Start by tracking your finances, using a monthly template. Use the income statement template (chapter 19) and mark down where every single penny goes for one full month! You may be unpleasantly surprised that you are spending $800/month on your car, $500 on meals, and $200 on coffee. However, unpleasantness can lead to potential areas of saving opportunities. Doing a monthly budget isn't supposed to ruin your fun; it is designed to help you decide where your money should be going to best achieve your viewpoints.

Believe it or not, it's easier to control how much you spend (the drains) rather than how much you make (the faucets). That's why the first principle of budgeting is to look at your expenses and make any possible modifications to incorporate your viewpoint funding - it's simpler and more economical than trying to switch jobs, beg for a raise, or train for a new career that could potentially earn you more money. As well, for those self-employed, some months your faucets will be gushing, other months you will have droughts! You will need to have enough savings to level out the higher with the lower months of income.

20.2 Barry Budgets a Beautiful Future

Barry decides to look at his expenses a little differently by calculating how much he needs to work to finance each expense. He estimates that he works 2,000 hours each year (40 hour work week, taking two weeks of vacation). His income is $50,000. Barry concludes that he makes $25/hour (annual income divided by 2,000 hours). Barry is astonished to discover that he needs to work 32 hours a month just to pay for his car ($800 is about the average monthly total cost to have a car in a Canadian city once lease/finance, gas, insurance, maintenance, and parking are added up). Barry decides to rent an apartment within walking distance to his clinic. Selling his car, Barry is now able to take every Friday off and keep his cash flow the same!

REST STOP *Dealing with debt:*

▸ **Pay off bad debt first.**

▸ **Shift your debt load.**

▸ **Assess your good debt: Are you paying the lowest interest amount of interest possible?**

20.3 Debt Management

Part of your budgeting strategy includes developing a plan for managing your debt. If you don't have debt, that's great! If you do, read on. There are many types of debt that you can have - some better and others downright sinister. Bad debt includes department store or credit card bills, which involve large amounts of interest and a blow to your credit rating if you don't pay the minimum balance. You want to avoid this kind of debt by paying your credit card bills in full, or at the very least paying the minimum balance until you can pay in full.

An example of friendlier debt is a mortgage. This is a long-term investment with a much lower interest rate. Paying off a mortgage can actually improve your credit rating and you will most likely get a high return on investment when you decide to sell.

Good debt is also often tax deductible or offers tax credits. So to summarize: house debt is acceptable and credit card debt is not. Shifting your debt load is the first step is to reducing your bad debt. This is accomplished by re-allocating your credit to less costly interest rates. For example, you can consolidate credit card debt into a demand loan, or transfer balances from a retail or department card to a credit card.

Once your bad debts have been addressed, you need to assess whether your good debt is as cost effective as possible. You may be able to find lower interest rates or shorten the amortization period of your mortgage. The easiest way to shorten an amortization is to pay your mortgage on a weekly or bi-weekly basis instead of monthly. In short, when you reduce interest costs, you are increasing your savings. Tighten your water bottle's leaks and store up your savings!

20.3.1 Danger Danger - Watch Out for the Loan Ranger

Canadians spend 103% of their incomes: we are actually spending 3% more than what we are making (Sauve, 2003)! Our expense drains are bigger, draining our cash flow savings. Sounds impossible? You are correct: one cannot continue to spend more than they make for long (despite what the advertisers on TV may say). Nowadays, there are more than enough companies willing to lend you money or allow you to buy things on credit in "easy" monthly payments. How many times have you been mailed credit card applications, home equity loan applications, or heard "Buy Now, Pay Later." Pay later indeed! Canadians are getting more and more into debt, and having compound interest working against them. Debt financing is a slippery slope and the best strategy is not to go there at all. A good rule of thumb to avoid debt financing is not to buy any personal items that you can't afford to pay for in cash. Use borrowed money only for your home or for investments or business expenses where the interest is tax deductible.

Debt Pyramiding is unfortunately becoming another buzz word. This is consolidating your credit cards into lines of credit. Freeing up your credit cards, you turn around, spend, spend, spend, and max them out again. Consolidating into an equity loan, you free up both your lines of credit and credit cards. However, you haven't learned your lesson: you get enticed by advertisers and max your lines of credit and credit cards yet again. Before you can say "Yes, I would like the extended warranty," you have a pyramid of non-deductible debt towering above you and draining your cash flow water bottle. Remember, in the land of debt financing, the lender (not the buyer) is king. Don't let the Loan Ranger get control of you!

REFERENCE

Sauve, R. (2003). *The current state of Canadian family finances*. Retrieved June 13, 2007, from http://www.vifamily.ca/library/cft/state03.html#Record_high

CHAPTER 21

Taxes

BRADLEY ROULSTON, BA, CFP, CLU, RHU

21.1 The Single Largest Cash Flow Water Bottle Drain

We all hate taxes, right? It's easy to forget that taxes pay for all our valuable Canadian social services, such as health care, road repair, and law enforcement. Although taxes benefit society, you can arrange your finances so that you aren't paying any more tax than you have to.

We live in a country with a progressive tax rate – meaning that we hit more expensive federal and provincial/territorial brackets of tax as our income rises. For instance, one person making $100,000/year pays far more taxes than a couple earning $50,000 each. Keep in mind that as you enter new tax brackets, only money earned in each new bracket is taxed at that rate; money in lower brackets is still taxed at those lower rates. You don't pay income taxes if your income is below approximately $8,800. Think of taxes as rain. Income below $8,800 is a sunny day; drizzle tax rain is income from $8,800 to approximately $33,000 at around 21%; rain soon gets more intense with 30% brackets; income higher than about $75,000 starts getting hammered with 40% rainstorms. The hardest tax rain in British Columbia is 43.7% for all income above $118,285 (Canada Revenue Agency, 2006). Talk about a tax rain monsoon!

The Olympic motto *Citius, Altius, Fortius*, is Latin for "Faster, Higher, Braver." Tax specialists have their own motto: "Avoid, Reduce, and Defer."

21.2 Avoiding Taxes

Believe it or not, there are ways to legally avoid paying income tax. Capital gains are avoided upon the sale of your principal residence (home). Income splitting to maximize basic personal amounts is another method. Other more advanced techniques could include the Small Business Exemption. Naturally, it is best to avoid paying a bill altogether over any other tax planning strategy.

21.3 Reducing Your Taxes

Taxes are reduced through deduction and credits. Deductions reduce your taxable income. For example, if you're making $70,000, but have $20,000 in tax deductions (RRSPs, a home business), you are only taxed on $50,000 of your income. At a tax rate of 35%, you've saved $7,000. Sound good? Well, tax credits are even more effective ways to reduce your taxes. That's because credits reduce dollar for dollar the amount of taxes that you pay. For example, if you have $5,000 in tax credits, your taxes are reduced by exactly $5,000. If your student loans are with the government, the interest on those loans generates a tax credit. Medical, disability, tuition, and donation credits are a few examples.

Our government often uses taxes as a way of controlling the population by steering purchase, investment, and business habits. Can you recall seeing an advertisement for tax credits if you buy more energy efficient furnaces, cars, etc.? That is their way of promoting cleaner air. The government encourages us to save for our own retirement, so that we don't rely on them. They invented the Registered Retirement Savings Plans (RRSPs). They encourage us to go back to school (Lifelong Learning Plan [LLP]), or save money for our children's education (Registered Education Savings Plans [RESPs]), or buy our first house (Home Buyers Plan [HBP]). Though whole new programs are sometimes introduced, offering deductions or credits are more common strategies. A good accountant will help you arrange your finances to take advantage of as many programs, deductions, and credits as possible, thus reducing the taxes that you need you pay.

The government encourages people to become self-employed. They do so by offering an assortment of business deductions. Essentially, anything that you spend money on as a cost of doing business or anything that helps you to realize a profit is a tax deduction. Expenses can only be used in the year that they are incurred, therefore, you want to maximize most of them in years when your income is higher and your tax rain is harder.

You should also separate your personal from your business records. Having a separate business bank account, line of credit, and credit card will help you. Any bank fees or interest charges to your business accounts are tax deductible. You will also save money on accounting fees if you can keep your records separate and clean.

21.4 Deferring Your Taxes

If you owed someone $10,000, would you rather pay them now or in 10 years? Deferring tax payments is the last slogan of tax planning. As long as your bill doesn't grow, it is best to put off paying tax until next year or in even longer. Waiting just one day from selling stocks that incurred capital gains from 31 December until 1 January, will defer taxes being paid for another full year! More strategic tax planning involves deferring tax to future years when your income is lower, thus both deferring and reducing tax.

An RRSP is a good example of a tax shelter. If taxes are rain, tax shelters (like RRSPs) are umbrellas – everything underneath is protected from the rain. There are two benefits to an RRSP: the reduction of current income and its tax deferred growth. There are many types of investments that qualify for an RRSP, from the traditional Guaranteed Investment

Certificate (GIC) to mutual funds. Any investment that is registered with the government as a retirement plan qualifies. The key consideration for an RRSP is whether its benefits outweigh those of non-registered investments. It is only logical that using your shelters and umbrellas as the rain comes down harder becomes more important (although at any time, a dollar saved is still a dollar earned). Using your RRSP umbrella is an amazing way to save for your retirement backpack. Try to maximize your RRSP contributions every year.

Another popular strategy for a reduction of taxable income is using a loan to invest. The annual interest on the loan is deductible against your earned income, similar to an RRSP contribution. The growth on the investment can often be taxed annually, so investigate the underlying investments and ensure that the tax is minimized. Swapping non-deductible for tax-deductible debt to write off the interest payments could also be an option.

A third area in tax planning is income splitting. This strategy reduces current taxes by lowering income tax levels and taking advantage of lower tax brackets. There are a number of possible strategies that can be employed to split incomes, from spousal RRSPs to establishing a corporation.

The fourth most common tax planning strategy is considering incorporation versus remaining self-employed. There are many pros and cons to incorporation. Advantages include lower corporate tax rates, business continuity, raising capital, liability protection, and advanced tax planning. Disadvantages include the cost of incorporating (+/- $1,500) and higher corporate accounting costs ($750/year or more). From a tax perspective, you need to save enough money in lower corporate tax rates to offset the higher legal and annual accounting costs. You save on corporate tax rates if you make more money than you spend. In a company's cash flow water bottle, these savings are called Retained Earnings. If you cannot save at least $15,000 in retained earnings each year, it is likely not cost effective for you to incorporate. Regulated health care professionals can only become professional incorporations.

It is important to meet with a Chartered Accountant and a Certified Financial Planner now to set up your affairs in the most effective manner. Don't keep waiting till the end of next year to ask "How did I do?"

Here are some of the more common business deductions:

- advertising
- allowance on eligible capital property
- bad debts
- business tax, fees, licenses
- association dues, memberships, and subscription
- communications & utilities
- capital cost allowance
- fuel costs

- delivery freights, couriers, and postage
- home office expenses
- insurance
- interest
- maintenance and repairs
- management and administration fees
- meals and entertainment (allowable part only)

- motor vehicle expenses
- office expenses
- supplies
- legal, accounting, and other professional fees
- property taxes
- rent
- salaries and benefits (including employer's contributions)
- travel

REFERENCE

Canada Revenue Agency.(2006). *Tax-rates*. Retrieved June 8, 2007, from http://www.cra-arc.gc.ca/tax/individuals/faq/taxrates-e.html#provincial

CHAPTER 22
Your Financial Knapsacks
BRADLEY ROULSTON, BA, CFP, CLU, RHU

22.1 Your First-aid Kit

22.1.1 The Art of Defensive Planning
Your first challenge on your financial hike is to fill your first-aid kit. There are a few necessities that go into this bag, and you must choose them wisely. You want to keep this bag as light and small as possible, packing only what you absolutely need. Packing too much will prevent you from packing enough in your other knapsacks. Packing too little can mean you don't get the help you need when the chips are down. Packing too quickly could lead to bad decisions. Delaying packing can mean you won't be allowed to pack anything at all.

The trick to packing a bag at just the right time that suits you best, is understanding your current needs and anticipating what your needs might be in the future. A written financial plan (guidebook) will illustrate how to most effectively and efficiently pack your first-aid kit.

22.1.2 Insurances

No one likes to think about the possibility of getting sick or injured. But it happens. In fact, injuries cost Canadians a total of about $156.9 billion in 1993 - roughly 22% of our gross domestic product (approximately $5,450 per person) (Herbert, 1998).

Health care professionals also run the risk of being sued. Even if you're confident in your abilities as a therapist, all it takes is one angry patient to file a suit and send you into debt - lawyers cost hundreds of dollars an hour.

That's why it's essential to make sure you have enough insurance to cover your medical and legal expenses, but not so much that you have to use most of your savings to maintain your coverage. Here is a list or basic insurances and why they're important:

Supplemental Health Insurance. This will help pay for drug and dental costs, and other unexpected treatments you might need. Certain costs might not be covered if they're associated with pre-existing conditions or illnesses you had before you applied for insurance. So it's important to buy insurance before there's a problem.

Disability Insurance. This will pay you a salary if you are too sick or injured to work. It's cheaper to buy "any occupation" insurance, but the more expensive "own/regular occupation" insurance will pay you if can't do your own job as a health care professional. "Any occupation" insurance won't pay you if you are able to do any kind of work that you are reasonably trained, educated, or experienced to do. Can you say, "would you like fries with that?" "Regular occupation" insurance will pay you if you can't do your own job, but will decrease your benefit if you choose to do another job while you're injured. You should expect to pay about 2% of your income for a comprehensive disability insurance policy. Protecting your ability to earn an income is essential and cannot be over-emphasized! Your ability to earn an income is most likely the largest faucet filling your cash flow water bottle – protect it!

Critical Illness Insurance. This insurance will provide a lump sum of tax-free money after the diagnosis of any one of approximately 23 critical illnesses (e.g., stroke, cancer, heart attack). Most people normally buy one or two times their annual income's worth of coverage. You can use the benefit to seek treatment outside Canada, hire a home care nurse, renovate your house to better accommodate your needs, or simply quit your job and travel.

Malpractice Insurance. This insurance will help cover legal costs in case you are sued for malpractice. This is mandatory for regulated health professionals to practice.

Life Insurance. This insurance will pay a lump-sum of tax-free money if you die to cover costs like funeral expenses, clear debts (mortgage), and provide money to support your family.

Home and Car Insurance. This protects large or expensive assets. Consider a higher deductible to lower your monthly premiums.

Linda is a healthy, middle-aged contractor. She's always been active and stayed fit, but one day she missed a step as she was leaving her house and fell. Linda's ankle snapped and she nearly lost her foot. Fortunately, she had disability insurance that supported her during the many months she couldn't work. However, her coverage wasn't quite enough: "Thank goodness I had the insurance, but I hadn't changed it to match my increasing salary over 15 years. What they paid me was a help, but just barely!"

The most important things to remember about insurance is to buy plans that you understand and that will pay you, and work with an insurance broker to make sure you're getting the most insurance for your money. Also, buy into health plans early before you develop too many pre-existing conditions that will be excluded if you wait to buy a plan after they arise.

22.1.3 Wills
Most people know what a will is, but very few understand its importance. Although the government automatically has a schedule of where your money is to go, this process can be long and family feuding is common. Also, you may not want your money going to where the government says - perhaps you aren't close with your family. Your will lets you dictate exactly who your money and assets go to if you die. Most family lawyers can help you write a will.

22.1.4 Powers of Attorney
There are two types of power of attorney. The first lets you choose someone to look after your finances if you are unable to. The other involves assigning someone to make decisions about your health. Powers of attorney become active as soon as you write them. You may want to give copies to your lawyer with instructions outlining when to activate your powers of attorney.

22.1.5 Line of Credit
Ah, the joy of credit - that spare cash that's not really yours. It's actually quite easy (and free) to open a line of credit at your bank. Having a line of credit means you are assigned a maximum amount of money you can borrow. The good news is you only pay interest on the money you actually use. Establishing a line of credit early is important. Once a crisis hits that leaves you strapped for cash, the banks will only lend you money at a very high interest rate - or they may not lend you money at all. So get as much credit as you can as early as you can by getting pre-approved - but don't use it unless you absolutely have to.

22.1.6 Good Credit Rating
Your credit rating is your reputation for borrowing money, so, of course, you want to establish a good one. A bad credit rating can mean saying goodbye to business loans, mortgages, car loans, department store credit cards, or even a phone line. Once you have a bad credit experience, the news spreads to all lending institutions, which are connected through a gossip group called the Credit Bureau. The Credit Bureau will also send collection agencies after you if you are well overdue on your payments. If you are seriously in debt, bankruptcy may seem like an easy way out, but it ruins your credit

rating and takes away from your financial independence. Try to manage your debt before declaring bankruptcy. We live in a debt financing society so keep your credit reputation in tip-top shape.

There are 5 simple tips to help you establish and keep a good credit rating:

▶ stick to a monthly budget;

▶ pay all minimum balances on time;

▶ only have one or two credit cards;

▶ get a line of credit and use it responsibly;

▶ call a credit agency (e.g., Equifax) and get your rating. There may be an error that needs correction.

22.1.7 Short-term Savings

It is important to have at least two or even three months of income saved in case of an emergency or opportunity. This could allow you to take time off work, change jobs, etc. Using your own saved money means that you won't have to borrow someone else's (like a bank loan, a line of credit, or a credit card) and pay back interest. Your savings should generate the best returns for you, but with no risk of losing any capital if there is a downturn in the markets. High interest savings accounts are often used here.

REST STOP *Be prepared with a well-packed first-aid kit:*

▶ **Insurance (supplemental health, disability, critical illness, malpractice, life, home and car).**
▶ **A will and powers of attorney.**
▶ **A line of credit and a good credit rating.**
▶ **Emergency funds that total two to three months of income.**

22.2 Your Dream Daypack

22.2.1 Dream the Possible Dream

We all have dreams - whether you want to buy a house, take a trip around the world, or have a huge wedding of Hollywood proportions, you'll need money to make your dreams a reality. That's where your dream daypack comes in. It's where you stash funds for long- and short-term life goals. Scary words like stocks, bonds, and mutual funds are your key to a house, a car, a trip around the world, or a killer stamp collection. You empty your sack when you've finished saving for something and begin filling it again for something else. So the dream daypack will change the most out of all your knapsacks because it will grow and shrink as you cash in on your dreams throughout your life. If you follow a few simple rules, your dream daypack will be easy to manage.

22.2.2 Dream Daypack Rules

To pack your dream daypack, first figure out which dreams are most important to you. You can save for several goals at once, but you may only be able to afford to put away money for one or two at a time. You also need to decide which of these goals are long-term and which are short-term goals are dreams that you plan to act on within five years.

Once you know which goals you want to start saving for, calculate how much your goals will cost and how much money you already have for them. Short-term goal funds should be lower-risk investments because if you're using the money within five years, there's no time to recover from market downs. A guaranteed investment certificate (GIC) is an excellent way to make your money work for you in the short-term because it guarantees growth. Keep your goals invested separately. That way you won't have to cash in the GIC for your child's education to gain access to the money you were saving for that $3,000 exotic bird you've always wanted. There are financial vehicles (e.g., Registered Education Savings Plans) that are designed to give your investments an extra boost. Talk to your trusted Financial Advisor about what programs or investment vehicles are best for each dream!

Keener Kathy deposits $1,000 into an investment account at age 25 and puts in $100/month until she turns 65. In total, Kathy has deposited $49,000. Average Al deposits $2,000 when he turns 35 and puts $200/month until he turns 65. At the end of Al's 35 years, he has deposited $74,000. Procrastinating Patricia waits until she is 45 to deposit $3,000 and tries to play catch-up by contributing $300/month until her 65th birthday. Patricia will have deposited just a little more than Al with $75,000. All three have wisely chosen an investment program that averaged 10%/ year. When all three are ready to retire at 65, Procrastinating Patricia has only $235,660. Average Al has $447, 467. Despite depositing the lowest amount, Keener Kathy has $600,294! When asked how this is possible, Kathy replied, "I had compounding coolness on my side. I didn't start with that much money, so I used time to my advantage."

REST STOP *Dream daypack basics:*

▸ Prioritize your goals.
▸ Invest your dream money so it grows.
▸ Invest short-term goal money in lower-risk funds.
▸ As your need for using the money gets closer, your investments should get more and more conservative/boring.
▸ Keep funds for different goals separate.

22.3 Your Retirement Backpack

Your retirement backpack needs to be big - really big. Let's say you live to be 90, but retire at 55. That means you'll have to support yourself for 35 years after you stop working. The government tries to pack some of this bag for you with the Canada Pension Plan (CPP) and Old Age Security (OAS). Unfortunately, many Canadians feel that they stand a better chance of seeing a UFO than their share of the CPP. Fortunately, there are a variety of ways to fill this backpack, from selling a business or property to cashing in investments, including Registered Retirement Savings Plans (RRSPs) and pensions. Work pensions, such as Hospitals of Ontario Pension Plan (HOOP), are also part of your retirement backpack.

22.3.1 Government Benefits

Despite their limitations, you are entitled to government benefits, such as the savings from your Canada Pension Plan that become available to you at age 65 at a maximum benefit of $844.58/month (as at 2005). You can cash in your pension plan funds as early as age 60, but your benefit will be 30% less, or your can access your funds as late as age 70, with benefits totalling 30% more. You will likely max out this benefit, which is funded by current contributors. If you are self-employed, you could pay the maximum yearly amount of $3,800+ (as at 2006), and if you are an employee, you split the cost evenly with your employer.

Another source of income after age 65 is Old Age Security (OAS). The Canadian government provides you with a maximum monthly cheque of $491.93 (as at 2006) if you've lived in Canada for 40 years or more, and a smaller benefit if you've lived in Canada for less than 40 years. However, if your income is over $62,114, your OAS benefits will be scaled back. Once your income is over $101,118, all of your OAS will be clawed back.

Good foresight involves planning so that you don't receive more than $62,114 of net income when you turn 65, hence retaining all of your OAS benefits. Use a pair of binoculars and plan not only for today, but for tomorrow as well.

REFERENCE

Herbert, M. (1998). Injuries cause significant economic burden. *CHIRPP News, 13* (March). Retrieved September 20, 2006, from http://www.phac-aspc.gc.ca/publicat/ chirpp-schirpt/13mar98/iss13h_e.html (consultd 20 September 2006).

CHAPTER 23
Investments
BRADLEY ROULSTON, BA, CFP, CLU, RHU

Investing is an essential part of building your dream daypack and your retirement backpack. You can invest by lending money (bank accounts, GICs, and bonds) or buying (equity and stocks). The government wants you to buy rather than lend, so you are taxed more on lending investments if your investments are outside your RRSP umbrella. Most people flinch when they contemplate buying investments such as a house, but you don't have to make large, risky purchases. Both lending and buying can be conservative or aggressive.

23.1 Investment Planning

There are four steps to proper investment planning:

1. deal with a professional;
2. invest without emotion;
3. allocate your investments according to your risk tolerance level;
4. regularly review your investments.

Dealing with a professional is important because it reduces the time you'll have to spend tracking your investments and making critical decisions. It will also remove most of the emotion from investing, which can lead to the classic mistake of buying and selling at bad times. You should plan to diversify your investments to minimize worries about market ups and downs.

23.1.1 To be or Not to be Balanced – That is the Question

Normally, it is easier to diversify and balance your portfolio by buying mutual funds, rather than individual stocks or bonds. Professional portfolio managers manage mutual funds. What they buy, invest, or sell is governed by the objectives of the fund (e.g., a Canadian balanced fund will invest in a combination of Canadian big companies and Canadian bonds). Your fellow investors in each mutual fund have a "mutual" objective. There are thousands of mutual funds to choose from and most have millions of dollars invested in about 100 companies at any given time! The investor pays a management expense ratio (MER) to pay for the management, selling, buying, reports, investment planner's commission, etc.; most fund MERs are +/-2.5%. Mutual funds are normally the easiest way for most investors to start. Most planners recommend sticking with mutual funds until your investment portfolio is more than $250,000; you can then diversify by using the services of a stock-broker.

Here are a few ideas to balance your investments portfolios:

▶ Choose a few "core" holding funds that best match your objectives and personality. This will keep you on track so you won't overweigh yourself in "hot picks" that can turn into duds.

▶ Consider global investments. These will increase your global exposure. Canada has recently had a strong economy, but still occupies only 3% of the world market. This will reduce your political and/or economic risk.

▶ Choose a balance of large, mid and small cap funds. Depending on market conditions, they will react differently.

▶ Combine growth with value style management. Growth management buys "popular" stocks while value management is like shopping only in the "discount" sections of the stock market.

▶ Opt for a variety of fund managers and investment firms. Managers will have good and bad years. Make sure that all of your funds are not handled by the same manager or management team

▶ Select a balance of equity and interest investments. Equities should do better in the long-run, however a balance is best. A general rule is 100 minus your age for a percentage of equity, minus interest weightings (e.g., if you are 35 years old, you may want 65% equities and 35% bonds).

- Make monthly contributions. Eliminate the timing game out of your investment purchases. Take pride that during bad months in the markets, you are buying investments on sale.

- Do the opposite of what your friends and colleagues are doing. When everyone is borrowing money to buy stocks, the market is probably too expensive. Likewise, when everyone is panicking and moving their money to GICs, it is time to get some deals.

- Be female – women make better investors. Generally speaking, women outperform men as investors by asking their financial advisors more questions and by being more patient with their investment strategy.

- Self-employed? Consider the better creditor protection that segregated funds offer if you are investing outside your RRSP umbrella.

- Work with a CFP (Certified Financial Planner). Take the next step in who you are getting your advice from. Better still, work with a CFP who understands the needs of health professionals, and who specializes with your age group or situation. Choose someone you like, trust, and is resourceful.

- Ask, Ask, Ask… don't just put your money into any old fund that seemed to do well last year. Take this list with you and add some of your own questions. Understand why and what you are investing in. It is your money that you worked hard for and your fate down the road!

23.2 Investment Success

Following your written financial guidebook accounts for 60% of you achieving your **Viewpoints** (life goals). This is just doing what your financial plan tells you to do (e.g., put aside $250/month for your retirement). Without worrying about where to invest your money, just doing what you are suppose to be doing accounts for the most likelihood of achieving your goals. Thirty percent (30%) comes from investing in the right asset allocation. **Asset allocation** might mean setting up your investment portfolio in: 10% cash, 20% Canadian equities, 15% international bonds, 20% European equities, etc. A proper financial questionnaire will help indicate what asset allocation you should have. This should be part of your full written financial plan. Lastly, only 10% of achieving your viewpoints actually comes from picking the right investment (though many salespeople may focus on this). Whether you invest in one investment firm's Canadian balanced fund or another, it will have little difference in the long run. What is important is putting enough money aside, starting early enough, and investing in the right general areas.

23.2.1 Dollar Cost Averaging

Set up monthly deposit/investment payment schedules. For example, every month, $400 comes out of your account and buys more units for your portfolio. Establishing habits is great for investor performance. It also eliminates trying to time the market yourself. Some months you will buy fewer units when performance is high, and other months, you will buy more units when performance is low and discounts are available. In the long run, you will get the average price of investments. Your money will also be invested and growing during the year instead of waiting to invest at year end. Don't forget to index your investment purchase amounts by inflation each year and as your salary increases!

3.2.2 Balancing Risk and Return

One rule that guides the risk level of your investments is how soon you need the money: the sooner you need the money, the more conservative or boring your investment should be. You also need to balance risk and return. Don't take a large risk if you don't think you'll get a higher return. For example, don't loan money to an unproven business for the same return provided by the government; the government is fairly safe - if the government can't pay back, they can either raise taxes or print more money!

Understanding risk is very important. There is no such thing as a "risk-free" investment. You could invest in a guaranteed income certificate (GIC) at 3%; however, once taxes and inflation are accounted for, you money could actually be shrinking (yikes!). Most people commonly assume losing their capital is the only form of risk. However, risk (properly defined) is the degree of uncertainty of achieving an expected rate of return. Risk can wear many disguises – sometimes we are totally unaware of the risks.

23.2.3 Risky Business

Here is a list of some areas of risk:
- risk of variability (investment asset values increase and decrease);
- risk of inflation (losing purchasing power);
- risk of loss of capital (asset value permanently decreases);
- risk of currency fluctuation (on international investments);
- risk of marketability (lack of secondary markets for trading);
- risk of poor results (selection without research/advice);
- risk of economic cycles (growth periods and recessions);
- risk by geographic or political regions;
- risk of liquidity (ease of converting to cash);
- risk of reinvestment (lost opportunities).

Working with a CFP and choosing great mutual fund managers, helps to alleviate many of these risks!

23.3 Where to Invest

There are many ways to invest your money such as:
- T-bills;
- GICs;
- Government and corporate bonds;
- Small, medium, and large capital Canadian companies;
- Small, medium, and large US, Asian, Pacific, European companies;
- Hedge funds;
- Resource funds;
- Individual stocks, bonds, or mutual funds.

You should invest in several areas as each investment always carries its own risks. This is called being **diversified**, or **balanced** in asset allocation. This is particularly important if you're investing in stocks, bonds, or real estate, which all fluctuate in "boom" and "bust" cycles. The markets go up (boom!) and then go down (bust!). Because no one can predict exactly when the parties will end, make sure you have investments in safer, more stable areas to compensate for investment losses.

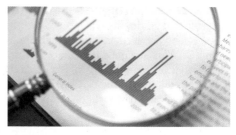

In addition, don't be a "rear-view mirror investor," investing in last year's best returns. This is like showing up late to a party after everyone else has had their fun. Your "late" investments will be expensive, so keep your emotion out of your investment plan and be smart. The golden rule is buy low, sell high – or buy when the cost to you is low and sell when your investments have increased considerably. Unfortunately, most Canadians do the opposite and buy high, sell low. Consider how many times you have heard "I am going to wait for the market to come up a bit before I invest." What this person is actually saying is "I know that there are bargains on right now, but I am going to wait until things get expensive again." We shop for clothes on sale, you should look for investments the same way. Learn to buy investments when they are out of fashion.

In your portfolio, you will have some investments that go up, others that stay about the same, others that will go down. Rebalancing means that you sell the ones that have gone up to buy ones that have gone down. You will re-establish your asset allocation and force yourself to always buy low, sell high.

Doris is happy with her portfolio. Her risk questionnaire and viewpoint objectives indicate that she should be invested in 5% cash, 15% Canadian fixed income, 5% international fixed income, 20% Canadian equities, 15% US equities, 10% international equities, 10% real estate, and 20% in tangible, specialty, and alternative. Six months later, Doris has met with her financial planner for her semi-annual review. Her objectives are still the same, however, over the six months, some investments did better than others. Consequently, her portfolio is now 5% cash, 14% Canadian fixed income, 3% international fixed income, 22% Canadian equities, 13% US equities, 14% international equities, 11% real estate, and 18% tangible, specialty, and alternative. Doris should sell some of those that have gone up and buy those that went down to re-establish her correct asset allocation. It is difficult for Doris to sell part of the winners to buy more of the ones that have performed worse. Doris takes her emotions out of her investment planning, remembers the motto "Buy Low, Sell High," and correctly rebalances her portfolio. Congratulations Doris! You have a bright future ahead.

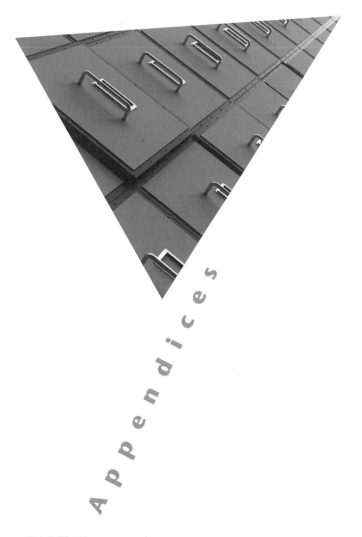

Appendices

PART III

Appendices

APPENDIX 1
The Business Plan Outline

Title Page

Table of Contents

Executive Summary
    (i)   Business Description
    (ii) Operations (ownership, management, implementation)
    (iii) Human Resources
    (iv) Marketing Opportunities and Strategies
    (v) Competitive Advantages
    (vi) Summary of Financial Projections

The Context
    (i)   The New Venture Definition (including "unique value") or the Business Definition
    (ii) The Background (why you, why this, why now)

The Strategy
    (i)   The Mission Statement
    (ii) The Vision Statement
    (iii) Key Features
    (iv) The "Go Criteria©" (key criteria for implementation)

The Environment and Market (Macro Analysis)
    (i)   Environmental Analysis (health care environment)
    (ii) Market Analysis (Ontario Private Sector Analysis – niche; market research, size of the industry, key market segments, key industry trends, industry outlook)

The Industry and Customers (Micro Analysis)
    (i)   Competitor Analysis (within and outside the profession)
    (ii) Customer Analysis (referral base, revenue sources, clientele)

The Products and Services
    (i)   Target Population
    (ii) Continuum of Care
    (iii) Scope of Services
    (iv) Methods of Service Provision
    (v) Range of Products

Management and Staffing
(i)   Ownership
(ii) Management Team
(iii) Professional, Adjunct, and Office Staffing
(iv) Labour Market Issues

The Location
(i)   Site/Venue (rationale, type, location, accessibility)
(ii) Space Design
(iii) Equipment

The Marketing Plan
(i)   Pre- and Post-opening Promotions, and Strategy and Evaluation Methods
(ii) Implementation: One Time, Ongoing, In-kind

Comprehensive Financial Statements (Years 1, 2, 3)
(i)   The Spreadsheets (expenditures, income)
(ii) Notes and Assumptions
(iii) The Balance Sheet
(iv) The Income Statement
(v)   Cash Flow Projections

Regulatory and Professional Issues
(i)   Relevant Legislation (health care, small business, human resource)
(ii) Professional Issues

Confidentiality and Recognition of Risks
(i)   Mitigation of Risks
(ii) Statement of Confidentiality

Appendices
1.   Detailed Financial Assumptions
2.   Demographic Data and Maps
3.   Contact Information and Glossary

A P P E N D I X   2
Independent Contractor Letter from
Canada Customs and Revenue Agency

Canada Customs
and Revenue Agency
Agence des douanes
et du revenu du Canada

March 8, 2004

Pamela C. Fralick,
Chief Executive Officer
Canadian Physiotherapy Association
410 - 2345 Younge Street
Toronto, ON,
M4P 2E5

Dear Ms. Fralick:

Subject: Template for self-employment contract for Physiotherapist

We are writing pursuant to a recent telephone conversation between Ms.Christine James, Membership Coordinator for the Canadian Physiotherapy Association (CPA) and Terry Bailey, Senior Programs Officer from Canada Revenue Agency (CRA). This letter will confirm that the contract template submitted by the CPA and the subsequent opinion expressed by the CRA is still valid.

As indicated in the letter sent by Rémi Côté, Manager CPP/EI Eligibility Division, on January 25th 1999, the parties who are going to use this contract will be in a contract for service relationship, which means that the physiotherapist signing the agreement will be considered self-employed for the purposes of the *Canada Pension Plan* and *Employment Insurance Act*, providing the template is a true reflection of the factual terms and conditions of employment.

We also want to take this opportunity to remind you that the terms and conditions of the contract must be strictly adhered to, more specifically clause 1.5 which stipulates that an appropriate fixed monthly cost must be charged to the physiotherapist for equipment and services provided by the clinic owner. Our rulings officer when requested to conduct a ruling, examine all the facts and conditions surrounding the employment in order to determine the employment status. This examination would also include the written contract between the physiotherapist and the clinic owner. It is for this reason that the factual situation must be consistent with the template that was reviewed by CRA.

.../2

Canada

R350 E (99)

Due to the evolution of the common law principles established by the courts that govern the analysis of employment status, you may wish to make changes to your 1999 contract template in the future. We will be pleased to look at your submission at that time and provide you with our comments.

For your convenience, we have enclosed a copy of the contract template and the letter from M. Rémi Côté.

Should you wish to discuss the matter further, please contact Terry Bailey at (613) 946-5348 or Jean-Pierre Lemay at (613) 946-5354.

Yours truly,

Danielle Héroux
Manager,
CPP/EI Eligibility Division
Canada Revenue Agency

Encl.

APPENDIX 3
Independent Contractor Contract Template

Canadian Association
Physiotherapy canadienne de
Association physiothérapie

National Office
2345 Yonge Street, Suite 410
Toronto, Ontario
M4P 2E5

Tel (416) 932-1888
Toll-free: 1-800-387-8679
Fax (416) 932-9708
E-mail: information@physiotherapy.ca

CANADIAN PHYSIOTHERAPY ASSOCIATION

PROFESSIONAL SERVICES AGREEMENT

(FOR USE BY INDEPENDENT CONTRACTORS)

P L E A S E   N O T E :

1. This form of contract may not be applicable to your particular working circumstances. In the event the form of contract does apply, please note that it has been drafted in general terms and may require changes in order to conform to your particular working circumstances. The form of contract should not be used prior to seeking independent legal advice with respect to your particular working circumstances.

2. Employment law is regulated provincially and therefore although the Canada Customs & Revenue Agency (CCRA) has stated that the form of contract reflects the status of the physiotherapist as an independent contractor, the form of the contract may not meet the requirements of independent contractor status under the employment legislation of your province. The College of Physiotherapists in your province may also have rules and regulations which will apply to the form of and use of the contract. You should obtain independent legal advice prior to using the form of contract to ensure that provincial requirements are met.

3. CCRA has advised that in the event that the form of contract applies to your particular working relationship and is used by you, should the terms of the contract not be adhered to in fact, CCRA will review your employment status.

4. In the event that you use the contract without seeking independent legal advice, by using the contract you agree that any and all losses, damages, liabilities, and all other claims of any nature whatsoever incurred by you relating to or in connection with your use of the form of contract ("Claims") will be your sole responsibility and you unconditionally and irrevocably release and forever discharge the Canadian Physiotherapy Association and its officers, directors, employees and solicitors and each of their respective successors, assigns, heirs, executors, administrators and personal representatives from any and all responsibility for such Claims.

CANADIAN PHYSIOTHERAPY ASSOCIATION
PROFESSIONAL SERVICES AGREEMENT

(FOR USE BY INDEPENDENT CONTRACTORS)

THIS AGREEMENT is made as of the _____ day of _____ ,20 __ .

BETWEEN: _____

*(the "Physiotherapist")

AND: _____

*(the "Proprietor")

WHEREAS the Physiotherapist is a member in good standing of the College of Physiotherapists of [insert province], and a member of the [insert province] Physiotherapy Association, having his/her principal residence at [insert address];

AND WHEREAS the Proprietor is * and operates a business at * ;

AND WHEREAS the Physiotherapist and the Proprietor are desirous of entering into an agreement pursuant to which the Physiotherapist shall provide his/her services to the Proprietor subject to the terms and conditions herein (the "Agreement").

NOW THEREFORE in consideration of the premises and the mutual covenants herein and other good and valuable consideration (the receipt and sufficiency of which is hereby acknowledged by each of the Physiotherapist and the Proprietor) the Physiotherapist and Proprietor hereto covenant and agree as follows:

1 RETAINER

1.1 The Proprietor hereby engages the Physiotherapist and the Physiotherapist hereby agrees to hold himself/herself available to render during the Term, at times mutually agreed to by the parties and attached as Schedule A , independent physiotherapy services to the best of his/her ability, upon the terms and conditions hereinafter set forth. Any amendment to Schedule A by either party shall require * (*) days written notice to the other party.

1.2 The Physiotherapist shall provide to the Proprietor those professional services hereinafter set out and more particularly described in Schedule "B" attached hereto (the "Services"). Notwithstanding the generality of the foregoing, the Physiotherapist shall not perform any act which is prohibited by law.

1.3 The Physiotherapist shall render the Services conscientiously and shall devote his/her best efforts and abilities thereto.

1.4 It is expressly agreed that the Physiotherapist is acting as an independent contractor in performing the Services hereunder. The Proprietor shall pay no workers compensation premiums or provide any health, disability, accident or life insurance to cover the Physiotherapist. The Proprietor shall not:

> **1.4.1** contribute on behalf of the Physiotherapist to the Canada Pension Plan;

> **1.4.2** deduct or withhold any amounts on account of employment insurance;

> **1.4.3** deduct or withhold any amounts on account of federal or provincial income taxes;

> **1.4.4** contribute to the Physiotherapist's professional licensing fees, memberships or professional association fees;

> **1.4.5** contribute to any fees or expenses relating to the Physiotherapist's professional development and continuing professional education;

> **1.4.6** reimburse the Physiotherapist for any automobile, travel or other expenses incurred by the Physiotherapist in the provision of the Services hereunder;

> **1.4.7** provide to the Physiotherapist any benefits other than as set out expressly herein.

1.5 The Proprietor shall provide to the Physiotherapist at a cost to the Physiotherapist of [* (*) Dollars per month], the equipment, supplies and secretarial and administrative services hereinafter set out and more particularly described in Schedule "C" attached hereto, which are necessary to enable the Physiotherapist to properly perform the Services.

2 TERM OF AGREEMENT

2.1 This Agreement shall commence on the * day of * 19* and shall continue for a period of * (*) year(s) from such date and shall terminate on the * day of * 19* (ATerm).

3 COMPENSATION

3.1 The Physiotherapist shall receive a consultation fee in the amount of * (*) Dollars per completed physiotherapy treatment, and in the amount of * (*) Dollars per completed physiotherapy assessment ("Consultation Fee"). The Consultation Fee shall be reviewed from time to time and may be adjusted by mutual consent in writing of the Physiotherapist and the Proprietor. Such agreed adjustment will be deemed to be incorporated into this Agreement.

3.2 All amounts payable under paragraph 3.1 hereof shall be paid to the Physiotherapist by the Proprietor within 15 days of the delivery by the Physiotherapist of a written report in the form agreed upon by the Proprietor and the Physiotherapist setting out all treatments and assessments conducted by the Physiotherapist during the preceding calendar month.

4 PROFESSIONAL STATUS

4.1 The Physiotherapist represents and warrants that:

4.1.1 The Physiotherapist is a member in good standing of the College of Physiotherapists of [insert province] and shall maintain his/her membership in the College of Physiotherapists of [insert province] in good standing and shall be, throughout the Term, entitled to practice physiotherapy in the Province of [insert province]. This representation and warranty shall survive the expiration or termination of this Agreement.

5 NON-EXCLUSIVITY

5.1 The Proprietor agrees that:

5.1.1 The Physiotherapist s Services hereunder are non-exclusive and the Physiotherapist shall be entitled to enter into contracts for service with other proprietors from time to time.

5.1.2 The Proprietor acknowledges that the Physiotherapist shall be responsible for providing the Services without instructions, supervision, or other interference from the Proprietor.

6 AMENDMENT OF AGREEMENT

6.1 This Agreement may be altered or amended at any time by the mutual consent in writing of the Physiotherapist and the Proprietor.

7 TERMINATION

7.1 This Agreement may be terminated at any time by written agreement of the parties.

7.2 The Proprietor may terminate this Agreement at any time upon * days written notice to the Physiotherapist.

7.3 The Physiotherapist may terminate this Agreement at any time upon * days written notice to the Proprietor.

7.4 Either party may terminate this Agreement at any time in the event of a material breach of the terms of this Agreement by the other party without any notice whatsoever to the other party.

8 GOVERNING LAW

8.1 This Agreement shall be governed by and construed in accordance with the laws of the Province of [insert province] and the laws of Canada applicable therein.

9 SEVERABILITY

9.1 The invalidity or unenforceability of any provision of this Agreement will not affect the validity or enforceability of any other provision hereof and any such invalid or unenforceable provision will be deemed to be severable.

10 ENTIRE AGREEMENT

10.1 This Agreement constitutes the entire agreement between the parties pertaining to the subject matter hereof. There are no oral warranties, representations or other agreements between the parties in connection with the subject matter hereof except as specifically set forth or referred to in this Agreement.

11 SCHEDULES

11.1 Schedules and other documents attached to or referred to in this Agreement are an integral part of this Agreement.

12 ASSIGNMENT

12.1 This Agreement shall not be assigned by the Physiotherapist but may be assigned by the Proprietor.

13 AGREEMENT BINDING

13.1 This Agreement shall enure to the benefit of and be binding upon the Physiotherapist and the Proprietor and their respective personal representatives, heirs, executors, administrators, successors and permitted assigns.

IN WITNESS WHEREOF this Agreement has been executed by the parties hereto.

SIGNED, SEALED AND DELIVERED

Date: _____   Per: _____   c/s

Date: _____   Per: _____   c/s2

Sample Schedule "C"

EQUIPMENT, SUPPLIES AND ADMINISTRATIVE SERVICES

The following equipment, supplies, secretarial and administrative services will be provided by the Proprietor to the Physiotherapist, at a cost of [* (*) Dollars per month]:

Equipment:

- Ultra sound
- Interferential
- Tens
- Muscle stimulators
- Mechanical traction
- Mobilization tables
- Etc.

Supplies:

- Hydrotherapy supplies
- Laundry
- Cleaning
- Office materials (charting paper, etc.)
- Etc.

Administrative and Secretarial Services:

- Client scheduling and rescheduling
- Client invoicing
- Collection of overdue accounts
- Overhead costs (office rent, heat, hydro, etc.)
- Equipment maintenance and repair
- Typing of correspondence
- Etc.

(PLEASE NOTE: This is provided as a sample Schedule "C", referenced in Paragraph 1.5, for illustration purposes only. Individual Agreements will vary depending on the type of equipment, supplies and administrative services that are provided by the Proprietor. The actual cost will be negotiated by the Proprietor and the Physiotherapist.)

A P P E N D I X 4
Small Business Glossary of Terms

ACCOUNTS PAYABLE: An account in the general ledger representing the amount owed by the business to its creditors on open purchases of goods and/or services.

ACCOUNTS RECEIVABLE: An account in the general ledger representing the amount due the business from its customers for goods and/or services sold on credit.

AMORTIZATION: The gradual reduction of debt by periodic payment sufficient to pay current interest and to eliminate the principal at maturity. This is also the term used for gradual reduction/writing off over a period of time in the book value of fixed or intangible assets, deferred charges and prepaid expenses, bond discount and bond premium, etc.

ASSETS: All of that which a business owns, including cash, merchandise inventories, real estate, equipment, supplies, copyrights, etc.

BALANCE SHEET: Statement of financial position of a business at a particular point in time; lists what is owned and owed.

BANK RECONCILIATION: A formal comparison of the balance in the checking account as shown on the bank statement with the balance of the cash account in the general ledger, at a given date.

CAPITAL: Available money to invest or the total of accumulated assets available for production. Put another way, your capital for going into business is the total of your property and money resources that you can make available for the business, and whatever you will need to live on while getting the business going.

CASH FLOW: Projections based on analysis of past operating experience, payment of obligations, and collection of receivables. This experience is applied to budgeted sales and costs for a future period in order to allow for repayment of loan obligations and to assure adequate working capital from earned income. Cash flow forecasts provide a fundamental financial-management tool for planning cash needs and ensuring adequate liquidity.

CORPORATION: A legal entity created under the laws of a state to carry on some business or other authorized activity. The principal distinction between a business corporation and other forms of business organization (i.e., proprietorship or partnership) is the fact that the liability of the owners is limited to the capital of the subject corporation.

DEPRECIATION: The decline in value of a limited-life tangible asset, such as a building, machine, vehicle, equipment, furniture, etc., due to age, and to the normal wear and tear of use. In general, depreciation assigns to a fiscal period a portion of the original cost of the capital cost asset.

EQUITY: The value of an enterprise or property that is owned; the actual value of the owner's financial interest in an enterprise.

FINANCING: The provision of operating funds to a business (by either loans or purchase of debt securities or capital stock).

FRANCHISE (FRANCHISOR, FRANCHISEE): A right or privilege to deal in a certain line or brand of goods and services. A franchising company (franchisor) is in the business of "selling" businesses or brands to small businesspersons. Usually, the franchisor and the businessperson who agrees (franchisee) enter into a binding contract where the franchisor supplies the product, materials and a certain amount of know-how, and the franchisee agrees to handle the product exclusively and run the business according to certain standards prescribed by the franchisor.

INCOME STATEMENT: A financial document that shows how much money (revenues) came in and how much money (expenses) was paid out. Subtracting the expenses from the revenues gives you your profit and all three are shown on the income statement.

INVENTORY: A list of assets being held for sale. If you are in retail business, the stock you have on the shelves is "inventory" but then so are your available supplies, goods received or stored, and any expendable items on hand.

LEASE: A contract between the owner (lessor) and the tenant/user (lessee) stating the conditions under which the tenant/user may occupy or use a property, a vehicle, equipment, etc.

LIABILITIES: The sum of debts or obligations of a business. Normally, the liabilities appear on the credit side of a balance sheet. This may be further broken down into current liabilities, long-term liabilities, etc.

LIABILITY INSURANCE: Risk protection for actions for which a business is liable. Insurance that a business carries to cover the possibility of loss from lawsuits in the event the business or its agents were found at fault when an action occurred.

LIMITED PARTNERSHIP: A legal partnership where some owners are allowed to assume responsibility only up to the amount invested. The idea for a limited partnership is that some investors may put up money for a business venture without being directly involved in its operation and so are not held responsible for the debts of the other partners beyond the possible loss of money they have invested.

MARKET: A place where products and services, and their competitive substitutes are brought and sold, an opportunity to sell, or the demand for goods and services.

MARKETING: Group of related business activities aimed at satisfying the demand for goods and services.

MORTGAGE: A deed, usually to real estate, given to secure the repayment of a loan made by the mortgagee (lender).

NET WORTH: Property owned (assets) minus debts and obligations (liabilities).

OBLIGATIONS: Any kind of indebtedness; an encumbrance or commitment.

PARTNERSHIP: A legal relationship existing between two or more persons contractually associated as joint principals in a business.

PROFIT MARGIN: The difference between your selling price and your costs. A lot of factors affect a profit margin, both inside and outside the business. A reasonable profit margin is necessary to remain in business.

PROFIT AND LOSS STATEMENT: A list of the total amount of sales (revenues) and total costs(expenses). The difference between revenues and expenses is your profit or loss. It is also called an "income statement."

RATIO: Denotes the relationship of items within and between comparisons of balance sheet items with profit-and-loss items; operating ratios are those derived from comparisons of items of income and expense.

RETAIL: Selling directly to the consumer. Selling in large quantities to dealers for resale is a "wholesale" activity, while selling in small quantities directly to people who will use the product is called "retail".

RETURN ON INVESTMENTS (ROI): In general, a concept used in business planning to determine the profit earned in relation to the value of the capital required to produce the profit.

SERVICE BUSINESS: A retail business that deals in activities for the benefit of others.

SMALL BUSINESS LOANS ACT (SBLA): A Canadian federal government program designed to help new and existing small enterprises obtain term loans directly from authorized lenders towards financing the purchase and improvement of fixed assets. The SBLA provides for the sharing of loan losses, if any, between the lenders and the federal government. Borrowing amounts may not exceed $250,000 and only businesses with less than $5 million in revenue qualify.

SOLE PROPRIETORSHIP: A business entity privately owned by a single individual.

TANGIBLE: Something that is real. Literally, "tangible" means that the thing is such that you can touch it, but the meaning for business is something that can be seen and evaluated.

Reprinted with permission from Kingston and Area Economic Development Company. (2005). Small Business Glossary of Terms [Brochure]. Kingston, Ontario: Peter Schell, Small Business Consultant.

APPENDIX 5
Small Business Resources

1. Government of Canada Business Start-Up Assistant: Available at: http://bsa.cbsc.org/gol/bsa/site.nsf/en/index.html

2. Government of Canada's: "Am I an Entrepreneur?": Available at: http://www.wd.gc.ca/tools/xindex_e.asp

3. Government of Canada's: Canada Business: Available at: http://canadabusiness.gc.ca/gol/cbec/site.nsf.

4. Canada Revenue Agency: Available at: http://www.cra-arc.gc.ca/menu-e.html

5. Business Development Bank of Canada: Available at: http://www.bdc.ca/flash.htm?cookie%5Ftest=1.

6. Industry Canada: Small Business Statistics: Available at: http://strategis.ic.gc.ca/engdoc/main.html

7. Canadian Bankers Association. (2004). *Getting Started in Small Business.* 3rd ed. Toronto: Author. Available at: http://www.cba.ca

8. Gerber, Michael E. (2004). The E-Myth Revisited: *Why Most Small Businesses Don't Work and What to Do About It.* 2nd ed. New York: HarperCollins Publishers (ISBN 0-88730-728-0).

9. Kerr, M. and Kurtz, J. (2004). *Canadian Small Business Kit for Dummies.* Mississauga: John Wiley and Sons Canada Ltd (ISBN 1-89441304-0).

Note: Access your profession's regulatory body Web site for provincial territorial resources including business practice advice, jurisprudence guidelines (including privacy legislation information), small business ethical standards (including conflict of interest guidelines), and other useful tips such as medico-legal report information.

APPENDIX 6
Using the Business Plan Spreadsheets

The spreadsheets are designed using Microsoft Excel and are interactive. The Standard Spreadsheet should be used for practices where the products are delivered by people (e.g. treatment, assessment, acupuncture) and/or if any goods are sold they are "off the shelf" goods (e.g. Theraband) and not ones manufactured in-house. For those business where a product is manufactured and sold to customers the "Cost of Goods Sold" spreadsheet should be used. For example if your business built and sold wobble boards as part of your product line, then the cost of supplies and labour for the manufacturing process need to be captured.

Both spreadsheets are designed to show three years worth of operations of your business. The spreadsheets will roll information from one year into the year following.

The spreadsheet has been designed to automatically calculate formulas and to carry the information to the three key financial sheets. All areas on the sheets shown in grey contain formulas. Do not try to change these cells.

The standard spreadsheet has 12 separate worksheets seen as tabs along the bottom of the page. The "Cost of Goods Sold" Spreadsheet has an additional two worksheets.

The Business Planning spreadsheets are designed to assist in preparing three key financial documents; the Cash Flow Statement, the Income Statement and the Balance Sheet. Each document has a unique purpose.

The Cash Flow Statement shows on a month-by-month basis the expenditures and revenues from your business. This document shows whether or not you have enough cash to cover the expenses on a month-by-month basis. It also shows the "Break Even" Point", that is the point in time when your business takes in more revenue than it pays out in expenses. The Break Even Point is a key consideration for bankers and potential investors in your business.

This worksheet contains information from each of the worksheets. Do not attempt to change any of the items on this sheet.

Areas to review include "the bottom line", Line 23 for Year 1, Line 45 for Year 2 and Line 67 for Year 3. These lines show the amount of cash available in your bank. If the number is low or negative you should consider taking out an Operating Loan. The other key lines are 22, 44 and 66. These lines show you the revenue minus the expense for that month. If the number is negative you spent more than you took in in revenues. The first month where that that number is consistently positive represents your "Break Even Point".

The Income Statement shows the profitability of your business. It takes gross revenues (total revenues not subtracting accounts receivable) and subtracts expenditures to give a "bottom line" number. If the bottom line is positive, your business is making money, it is profitable. If the number is negative then your business is not profitable at that point in time.

The Balance Sheet shows the value of your business at a single point in time, typically the end of a financial period like a fiscal year. The Balance Sheets shows Assets, things your business owns, and Liabilities, debts that you have to banks and shareholders. The Balance Sheet is so named because it will always balance, that is the assets will always match the liabilities. The key to this balance is the "Owners Equity" line. The Owners Equity is the value of the owner or shareholder stake in the business. If it is negative then the owners have lost value in the business over the period of time shown.

Title Page Worksheet
Enter the name of your business and this will be carried over to each of the pages in the spreadsheet.

Revenue Worksheet
To complete the Revenue Worksheet you will need to have decided on:

▶ what products you will offer,

▶ what price you intend to offer them at,

▶ how many customers per product you expect per month.

The spreadsheet is pre-loaded with eight products. Click on the "Product 1" cell and enter the product name. A product is any service or item your business will provide with a unique price. Products can be services like assessments or generic treatments or they can be specific treatments like acupuncture or massage therapy. If you plan to offer assessments and treatments to special populations and have a special price (e.g. for workers compensation patients) you should enter these as separate products. If you plan to sell items (e.g. Theraband, wobble boards) these should be listed as separate products

The Revenue Sheet also automatically calculates how much money you will receive per month for work performed in that month. The Spreadsheet assumes that you will receive 80% of the revenue that you billed in the month it was billed and the remaining 20% in the following month. This 20% is referred to as "Accounts Receivable".

Supplies Worksheet
To complete the Supplies Worksheet you will need a catalogue for both clinical supplies and office supplies. You will need to determine:

▶ how many customers you plan to serve,

▶ how many supplies each will require.

Enter the amount of supplies you expect to use over the course of 12 months.

The Supplies Worksheet is pre-loaded with many common supplies used by rehabilitation clinics. Delete supplies that you will not use. Enter the quantity of supplies and the price including the appropriate taxes. The spreadsheet is designed to have office supplies purchased every six months and clinical supplies purchased every three months.

Fixed Assets Worksheet

To complete this page you will need to decide:

▶ what types of equipment you plan to acquire for the practice,

▶ whether or not you plan to purchase the equipment or lease it.

There are two types of assets: capital, those that are over a certain value ($500 is a common value used) and non-capital, those that are under this amount. Capital assets that you purchase need to be depreciated. This reflects the fact that as years go by the asset drops or depreciate in value. The spreadsheet assumes that the asset will depreciate to $0 value over 5 years. Non-capital assets are not depreciated. The spreadsheet is pre-loaded with some common assets. Delete those that you will not use.

Banking Worksheet

To complete this worksheet you will need the following information:

▶ The amount of any money that you or your partners will put into the business up-front,

▶ The amount of any Term Loans that you may require from a financial institution to help will financing your start up,

▶ The amount of any Operating Loans that you may need during the year to maintain a positive bank balance,

▶ If you plan to purchase property, the amount of any Mortgage and the amount of a down payment,

▶ An idea of what type of business banking plan you intend to acquire,

▶ An idea of how customers will pay for your services (e.g. cash, interact, credit card) and how many customers will use debit or credit cards.

If you plan to put some of your own money into the business up-front, this amount should be shown in cell D7. Also enter any money that others may give you for the business IF they do not plan to charge you interest on this money.

It is very common to require a Term Loan to assist in offsetting the one-time costs of starting a business. You will have to determine how much money you may need to borrow by reviewing how much equipment you require, if renovations are needed to your practice location, and how long it will take for your practice to become profitable.

Once you have determined how much you need to borrow enter this amount in Column B in the appropriate month (usually the first month). You also need to determine the term or length of the loan and the interest rate. You will need to use a loan calculator (most banking web sites offer them) to determine the principle payments and the interest payments separately. Monthly principle payments are shown in Column C and the monthly interest payments are shown in Column D.

You will need to determine if you require an operating loan at some point during the year. An Operating Loan is typically used on a short term basis to cover expenditures in months where revenues may be down or expenditures may be up. Operating Loans may also be called a Line of Credit or Overdraft Protection. They are typically short term in nature and are repaid quickly. Review the Cash Flow Sheet to determine if there are months when your cash balance would be $0 or negative. This means that you do not have the cash to meet the next months expenses.

Enter the amount of an Operating Loan in Column E. Again use a loan calculator to separately determine monthly principle and interest payments. Enter these amounts in Columns F and G.

If you plan to purchase a property for the practice enter the purchase price in cell D9. If you are making a down payment on the property enter this amount in the appropriate month in Column K. The amount mortgaged (purchase price minus down payment) goes in the appropriate month in Column H. Use a loan calculator to determine the separate principle and interest payments and insert these in Columns I and J.

You will need to work with a financial institution to establish bank accounts for the practice. Most financial institutions offer packages for small business which incorporate checking accounts, payroll services, insurance, loans, etc. You will pay a monthly amount for these services. Enter this monthly amount in Column L.

If you plan to offer your customers the option of using a debit card or a credit card you will need to determine how much you will pay a financial institution for the required equipment and computer linkages. Typically this amount is based on a percentage of the amount being processed. Review your Revenue Worksheet and determine how many of the customers will use debit or credit cards and what the value of the amounts will be, apply the percentage to this amount.

Utilities and Property Worksheet

To complete this worksheet you will need to know:

▶ What utilities you may be responsible for paying

▶ Rent expenses

▶ Renovation costs

▶ Property taxes

▶ Property insurance

The worksheet is pre-loaded with 5 common property expenses, click on the expense to change them to those that are applicable to your practice.

Wages Worksheet

To complete this worksheet you will need to know:

▶ How many employees you plan to have,

▶ How much you plan to pay each employee,

▶ If you plan to have independent contractors affiliated with your practice,

▶ The appropriate deductions for each employee (e.g. Employment insurance, CPP),

▶ Whether you will offer benefits to your employees and the cost of the benefits.

The worksheet is preloaded for 8 employees. Click on the cell and replace the "Employee 1" etc., with the type of employee (e.g. Physiotherapist 1). To complete the cell you will need to determine the monthly wage cost of that employee. The monthly wage cost may be a determined by multiplying an hourly wage rate times the number of hours worked or a flat monthly rate. You will be required to deduct and submit to the government certain legislated amounts for Employment Insurance (EI), Canada Pension Plan (CPP) and possibly others depending on the jurisdiction of your practice. For certain deductions there is an employee portion and an employer portion. For the purposes of this spreadsheet only include the employer portion as this is a cost to your business. Many of the deductions are calculated as a percentage of the wage. The worksheet is NOT designed to calculate this given the wide variety of amounts that vary by jurisdiction. Enter the amount for each deduction.

If you choose to offer benefits to you employees enter the cost to you. Benefits can be a percentage of wages or can be a package deal.

If you plan to pay yourself as an employee then enter yourself as one of the employees at the appropriate rate.

If you plan to have independent contractors working in your practice you need to decide how they will be paid. One option is to enter them as an employee and show the amount they will be paid per month. Independent contractors pay their own EI, CPP and benefits. If they are to be paid a percentage of the amount of work they generate then it is more appropriate to show their revenue as a Product on the Revenue Worksheet and the Payment to the contractor as an expenditure on the Operating Expenses Worksheet.

Marketing Worksheet

To complete this worksheet you will need:

▶ A marketing plan with the various elements identified and costed.

A marketing plan can consist of many items. The spreadsheet is pre-loaded with 7 commonly used marketing tools. Click on each one and replace with the appropriate heading.

Operating Expenses Worksheet

To complete this worksheet you will need:

▶ Professional and practice insurance costs

▶ Legal expenses

▶ Accounting expenses

▶ Independent Practitioner payments (if appropriate)

▶ Licenses and permit expenses

▶ Laundry/linen expenses

▶ Housekeeping expenses

This spreadsheet contains two columns that are brought forward from other worksheets they are shown in grey. Do not change these columns. The worksheet is pre-loaded with 4 additional categories, click on then and enter the categories appropriate to your practice.

On the "Cost of Goods Sold" version of the spreadsheet there are two additional worksheets.

Cost of Goods Sold Worksheet

To complete this worksheet you will need:

▶ The cost of each component of each product you intend to manufacture.

The spreadsheet is pre-loaded with 4 headings for product components. Enter the monthly expenditure for each component of your products.

Overhead Wages and Benefits Worksheet.

To complete this worksheet you will need

▶ How many employees you plan to have,

▶ How much you plan to pay each employee,

▶ The appropriate deductions for each employee (e.g. Employment insurance, CPP),

▶ Whether you will offer benefits to your employees and the cost of the benefits.

This worksheet is only to be used for employees who are engaged in the manufacturing of your products. If you have employees who do some manufacturing work as well as other work in your practice you need to determine how much time is spent on each task (e.g. 50/50) and show the wage and benefit costs on the appropriate worksheet.